I'M SPEEDING BECAUSE
I HAVE TO POOP!

I'M SPEEDING BECAUSE I HAVE TO POOP!

First Book in the "Dumping with the Derksen's" Series

Shawna J Peterson

Copyright © 2015 Shawna J Peterson

All rights Reserved

ISBN: 0994869703
ISBN: 9780994869708

Published by: Shawna J Peterson, Winnipeg, Manitoba
(with Createspace, an Amazon company)

Copy Edited by: Blair Friesen and Christian Abadia

First Printing: November 2015

Acknowledgements

FIRST AND FOREMOST, I would like to thank my amazing husband, David Peterson, for giving me the time and space to work on this project. Babe, I know it was a huge sacrifice to be forced out of the house and go on weekend ice fishing trips with your buds in order for me to have a quiet environment to write. Seriously, though, your love, words of encouragement, and unwavering support have made this journey easier. Your excitement when you recalled funny stories that generated new ideas for the book were an endorsement of your approval, which was crucial to me. You are the light of my life, and the person with whom I share my most deep and intimate thoughts. Thank you baby! I love you more than you'll ever know.

I would also like to thank my other family; not all of whom are mentioned in this book. While this first edition is primarily about the escapades of the Derksen family, I am incredibly blessed to also be a part of the Peterson family. This small, but warm and loving family, are the best in-laws one could ever hope for. Mom, Hank, Z'Anne, Jim, Cheyenne, Jamie, Harvey and Sunny D (aka Deanna): Thank you for always accepting me "as I am", even though my humour and sense of spirit may be a little over the top at times. You've all impacted my life in some form or another, and I consider myself very fortunate to a part of this awesome family. I love you all!

A big thank you to the following individuals who gave me **permission** to include their poems and experiences: My immediate family Dave and Eric Peterson, Dad (Peter Derksen), sisters Nancy Luff and June Tymm, brothers-in-law Barry Wiebe, Jim Stojan, and Harvey Peterson, as well as nieces and nephews Jackie Kennedy, Robyn Tymm, Matty Luff, Jarrod Tymm, Jay Kennedy, Brad Sarna, Cheyenne and Jamie Moore. I love you so much and you all mean the world to me! Also, aunts and uncles Mary Thiessen, and Ben and Helen Dyck; cousins Blair Friesen and Virginia Froese, and of course, my dear friends, Joan Burdz, Susan Backer, Marlene and Daryl Michaluk, Carole and Ray Dupuis, Pat McBride, and Larry and Llowyin Weselake. Your friendships have enriched my life and I am blessed beyond measure to have known each of you. To my past and present colleagues, Roger Beebe, Vaughn Simpson and Blair Raitt as well as Winnipeg Blue Bomber buddies Billy and Jeff: You've injected fun memories that will be fondly remembered for years to come!

My mom and brother are in Heaven but I know they would have approved their stories being included. When I close my eyes, I can hear both of them laughing out loud at some of the experiences being told in this book.

I need to express a very special acknowledgment to my best friend, Teresa Dyck. We met as a Derksen and a Moerland in grade 8 and have remained friends throughout our childhood, teenage years, young adulthood, and pre-retirement seasons. Even though our last names have changed, our friendship has not. We're still happily married to our true loves and have had families of different structures. You and Ray, along with your beautiful boys, Trevor and Mason, uphold the family values of our generation. I love you so much and have enjoyed making amazing memories with you over the past 36 years. Thanks for allowing me to share a select few of them with others. I'm looking forward to making more memories in the years to come!

A heartfelt thanks goes out to my dear friend, Kathleen McCarthy, whom I met while working for Transport Canada. Kathy taught me how to thumb my nose at the world and laugh at myself when it seemed like life was crumbling around me. Her lesson to me was to not take life too seriously, live each day to the fullest, and be grateful for what you have – not what you don't. Kathleen suffered serious health issues a few years ago and still, she is impacting people and enriching the lives of her friends and caregivers. Thank you for coming into my life, my friend! You are always in my heart and prayers.

Thank you to my pseudo-brother, Blair, for both suggesting the title of the book and co-editing the manuscript with his friend, Christian. While neither of them are professional writers or editors, I was thrilled that they were willing to spend a great deal of time working on this project, which is so near and dear to my heart.

The subtitle is credited to my second cousin's wife, Tessa, who came up with the title *Dumping with the Derksen's*. I knew immediately that I was going to use this catchy phrase in some capacity for this book.

I would be remiss if I did not acknowledge my two bosses, Nadine Stiller and Cameron Buchanan, for allowing me the time away from work to focus on this project. Without the extended period of leave, this book would have taken many more months to complete.

Last, but certainly not least, I owe it to my Lord and Savior, Jesus Christ, for giving me the courage to write this book, the wisdom to include acceptable stories (even though some of them are borderline), and the patience required to move through each step of the process with care and diligence. I've tried very hard to make this book respectful while reflecting my individuality and humour. I'm very thankful for the gift of creativity, and the principles of perseverance, and commitment!

I truly hope I have not omitted anyone. Please forgive me if I have.

Introduction

LOOKING BACK, I'VE always been interested in writing stories. While I've never considered myself to be a technical writer, family and friends always enjoyed my ability to tell a story.

Going back to my teenage years, I became involved with our high school newspaper, *The Oak Park Vibes*, writing editorial articles, and assisting in the production of the newspaper. I also took an interest in the Oak Park literary magazine, which consisted of short stories. My mentor, the coolest English teacher ever, Mr. Gerry Archer was brilliant and a ton of fun. Everyone loved his English and Journalism classes, along with his unique teaching style.

After high school, I took a creative writing course at Red River Community College and then strayed from the literary field entirely.

In recently chatting with Marlyn Nicholson, a childhood friend whom I hadn't seen in over 21 years, I was reminded that I was writing books in grade 3. I don't recall those days, however, I suppose those deep-seeded interests never really go away, do they?

This non-chronological book has been verified by the individuals showcased in each story and is 100% accurate. The names have not been changed to protect the innocent. We're all guilty of doing silly things, making questionable decisions, over-indulging, and being downright goofy from time-to-time!

I wanted the stories and poems to be funny, positive, and relatable. I hope you find it to be at least one of those!

This is a very personal look at my fun and quirky family, as well as friendships I've developed over the past 40 years.

Enjoy!

Table of Contents

	Acknowledgements..................... v
	Introduction........................ix
Chapter I	Introducing the Derksen Family.............. 1
Chapter II	Becoming a Peterson..................... 59
Chapter III	Just Me 97
Chapter IV	My Bestie, Teresa...................... 111
Chapter V	More Of My Fabulous Friends and Family........ 143
Chapter VI	Concerts / Live Performances 189
	Thank You!........................ 193

Chapter 1

Introducing the Derksen Family

Then and Now

Upper Photo - From top left to right: Mom, Nancy, June, Dad, Vince, and Shawna (1969)

Bottom Photo – from left to right: Shawna, Dad, Mom, June, Nancy, and Vince (2008)

Meet Our Folks: Peter and Sue

FOR NANCY, JUNE, SHAWNA AND VINCE
(Written by our Mom)

Before you were conceived, we wanted you
Before you were born, we loved you
Before you were an hour old, we would have died for you
This is the miracle of Love

We found this verse on a small piece of paper in the Family Bible after Mom passed away in November 2013

Our beautiful, loving mother, Sue (1940 – 2013), with our handsome and witty dad, Peter

I'm Speeding Because I Have To Poop!

Dad's 65th Birthday
(Written by Shawna)

The family gathers around in total dismay
As we celebrate a very special "65th" birthday
To some he's Peter or Papa, but we call him Dad
He's funny and witty and occasionally "bad" (but in a good way)

He's known for his humor and jokes all alike
If you don't like them, well then "take a hike"
He's a generous soul and willing to help when needed
But don't get on his bad side or this gentle man can get over-heated

He's open to suggestions from time to time
But he's stick to his motto "You have a right to your own opinion…
just as long as it agrees with mine"!
Our holidays were fun and memories made
Whether we were camping or traveling, we had it "made in the shade"

His schnicker of choice is coke and rum
But his favorite appetizer has got to be Mom
He's absolutely adorable in his pink bunny suit
In his Halloween costumes, he always looks so cute

He's totally fun and loves to party
His infectious laugh is heavy and hearty
He's now semi-retired and is starting to slow down
His work week is shorter, so he has more time to "clown around"

He now has time to bowl once a week
He loves the activity, but says he scores wreak
He has recently started to make homemade wine
Well, Dave actually makes it, but Dad bottles it just fine

Shawna J Peterson

He loves spending time with family and friends
Sometimes we think his social life simply never ends
He worked hard all these years to give us a good life
He's done a fine job as we all turned out "all right"

So here's to our Dad on this very special day
With a whole lot of love
HAPPY "65TH" BIRTHDAY!!

Dirty Dentures

My Mom's birthday celebration weekend started on a Friday and ended on a Saturday night.

My sister Nancy had flown in from Calgary to celebrate my Mom's milestone birthday. With the rest of us kids living in Winnipeg or surrounding areas, mom had all of her kids for the weekend and couldn't have been happier.

The first event was an intimate family gathering at my sister's house with Mom and Dad, us 3 kids, and my husband, Dave. Unfortunately, my brother, Vince, and his wife were unable to make it. We met at my sister June's house for an evening of nibbles, schnickers, and Wii competitions.

My mom's big party with her family and friends was scheduled for the next day.

Friday evening was fun, loud, and a good time was had by all as we took turns Wii bowling for hours. We also enjoyed a few beverages, especially my Dad.

Around 10:30pm, June escorted my folk's home, even though they lived only eight mobiles homes down from her. When she returned to her place, she indicated that mom was very upset with dad because he was so hammered (which he rarely gets) and she was afraid that he was going to be hung-over for her big party on Saturday.

A few moments later, the phone rang. I tried to answer the phone but it just kept ringing because I forgot to press the 'TALK' button so the phone wouldn't connect. Normally, that wouldn't be funny but when you've had a few bevvies, everything is funny. So I threw the phone over to Nancy, who was also laughing hard. When Nancy finally hit the 'TALK' button, she was still laughing and could barely speak. All she heard was Mom crying.

As I write this, I feel bad for our behaviour. However, trust me when say that we were simply out of control and couldn't stop laughing. It was like something had taken over our bodies and we couldn't reel it in.

Nancy, who you will read about shortly, is the angelic sister. You know, the one that the rest of us were always measured against. She almost never upset or disappointed Mom and Dad.

Back to the story

Nancy tried to repress the laughter, but she already had the giggles and she just couldn't stop. When Nancy was finally able to compose herself, she was listening intently and repeating what Mom was telling her.

Nancy wasn't speaking clearly to say the least, but we did understand two words that she said: "teeth" and "toilet"

Wowzers!! We fell to the floor and laughed so hard we thought we'd pee ourselves.

My mom was so mad at Nancy that she hung up on her! For my mom to do that, she must have been so upset, but we couldn't stop laughing.

We looked at June and said, "You gotta call her back because none of us can."

After banishing us to the back of the mobile home where Mom wouldn't be able to hear our laughter, June called Mom back. Unfortunately, we were laughing so hard (I mean hysterically) my husband, Dave, suggested that June go outside to talk to her.

When she came back in, we all reconvened in the living room and she proceeded to tell us that dad had thrown up so hard; his false teeth went down the toilet.

What? Here we go again! Nancy and I fell to the floor and rolled on the living room carpet holding our stomachs. In 21 years, my husband has never seen me laugh that hard.

Obviously none of us girls could help my Mom, therefore Dave was "volun-told" to go over and see exactly what the situation with Dad's teeth was.

Dave arrived at my folks place to discover Mom still crying and dad passed out in their bed with his teeth firmly stuck in the toilet.

My mom explained that she didn't see the teeth in the toilet through all the tissue, toilet paper, and puke. If she *had* seen them, she certainly wouldn't have *flushed and plungered* repeatedly until the toilet was clear! It was only then did she see his teeth, stuck to the bottom of the toilet! The teeth were suctioned to the drain hole (the one that you see at the bottom of the toilet bowl). Dave tried to gently pry them off but they were firmly stuck. After asking Mom's permission, Dave used both hands and yanked them out of the toilet. Oh man, THEY BIT HIM (left teeth marks and drew blood too)! Dave's hand was bleeding but that was the least of the problem. Dad's teeth were now in two pieces. Yep, they broke in half!

My mom was concerned about Dave's hand, of course. However, she also pondered the thought of her toothless husband at her birthday party the next day. No, this was definitely not the birthday weekend she had imagined.

After Dave cleaned his bite marks and bandaged up his hand, he asked mom if she had any glue for Dad's teeth.

At this point, dad had woken up a little and overheard part of Dave and Mom's conversation. He rubbed his top and bottom lip together and only then realized he didn't have his teeth in his mouth. He stayed silent and pretended to still be passed out. That was a very smart move on his part, as Mom would have torn him a new one right then and there.

Dave glued the teeth perfectly and returned to June's to give us an update.

Nancy, June, my niece, Robyn, who had arrived home, and I waited patiently for Dave to return to give us the status on Dad's teeth and Mom's sanity.

As soon as he walked through the door, we all looked up and with no words spoken, I gave him the thumbs-up with the assumption that everything went well. Sadly, Dave just put his head down to his chin and shook it back and forth. That sent us back down on the floor laughing again. Seriously, my abs never had a better workout!

Dave explained what happened and we completely lost our minds. My sister may have peed her pants at this point, but I'm not entirely sure of that.

While we honestly felt really bad for Mom, the story was just too funny and we could not stop laughing.

Thankfully, Dave did such a great job on his teeth that my dad was able to wear them for my mom's birthday party on Saturday.

While mom didn't talk to dad for most of the day, they were back on speaking terms by late afternoon and had a wonderful time at her party. In fact, that evening she told the story several times and laughed about it too.

Left Photo: Demonstration on where Dad's dentures were stuck
Right Photo: Dad's party trick of chattering his upper dentures

Mom's Birthday
(Written by June)

Happy birthday dear mom
Happy birthday to you
You're one of a kind
Which means you are very special too

You spend hours cooking
And baking as well
And you share all your goodies
With all those great smells

You take time for your family
As well as your friends
And take well-deserved naps
When your kitchen duties end

One day your daughter#2
Will really surprise you
And will bust out the canning supplies
And pickles for you too!!

It is time for us to celebrate
Your birthday with you
So pour yourself a rye
And we'll drink champagne with you!!

Faked Her Out

Mom always made her kids and grandkids huge goodie bags around Christmas time. It would consist of an assortment of cookies, squares, cinnamon buns, butter tarts, matrimonial cake, cabbage rolls, perogies, and the list goes on. We all knew how much money it cost for these ingredients and I felt bad that she put so much work into it, only to give it all away to her children and grandchildren.

We convinced mom to start making some money from her gifting in the kitchen and she started a small side-business called Sue's Baking. I created a menu of baked goods and other popular food items, which I brought to my office. I always kept Mom very busy with orders, especially her cinnamon buns, which were ordered by the dozens. While the orders kept her busy, she still insisted on giving Christmas goodie bags to us kids and grandkids.

I knew that mom would never accept any money from me for a personal order, so I had to come up with a solution to support her business in a more creative fashion. I placed an order for an assortment of everything on her menu and randomly picked a name of an employee who had placed an order in the past. Surely, mom wouldn't give it a second thought! That person was Blair Raitt. I gave her the cash for the order and specifically asked her to deliver the goods to our home and assured her that I would bring it to work for Blair. After all, I did go to work every day and it was convenient to simply drop the order off on his desk. Little did she know the stuff was going straight into my freezer!

I'm not sure why, but Mom and Dad decided to make some deliveries on their own and went directly to my work. This was in the day where all employees had to take a one-hour shift at the reception desk until a permanent receptionist was hired. As luck would have it (or should I say as *un*-luck), Blair happened to be sitting at the reception desk when Mom and Dad arrived with "his" baking. He said he hadn't recalled placing an order but would take the items and talk to me when I returned.

When I got back from lunch, there were two messages on my desk. One from a colleague and the other from Blair:

1. "Your folks were here but you were on lunch."
2. "My baking order is here, but I didn't order anything… call me."

My mouth dropped, as I hadn't told Blair that I had used his name on the fake order.

Before I had a chance to call Blair, I saw him walking towards my workstation with his hands out, palms up and shoulders shrugged (indicating, "What the heck?"). I was beet red and busted!

After a quick synopsis from Blair with respect to my parent's visit and what seemed to be a lame explanation in return from me, he said to me, "For Pete's sake Shawna, feel free to use my name anytime, but you need to tell me so I can cover for you."

"How would I of known they would deliver it straight here when I asked them to drop it off at my house?" I explained. I acknowledged that I could have sent him an email at the very least, but honestly did not think they would come and personally deliver the order.

At this point, the deed is done and we were now in recovery mode. What *was* I going to do? I had to call my folks back as my dad had already called again after he returned home from the delivery. I was starting to sweat as I can't lie to save my soul and I knew I had to make something up or my mom would have returned the money and I certainly didn't want that to happen.

After a brainstorming session with Blair, we came to the conclusion that something simple was the best option. I called my mom and dad back and explained that the order had come from Blair's wife and not him directly, which was why Blair wasn't expecting the delivery. Mom and Dad never mentioned it again.

During a visit with my folks a few years ago, we were reminiscing about my mom's side-business and I decided it was time to fess-up. I guess I really did fake her out as both my parents could barely remember the incident. My guilty conscience plagued me for years and they didn't think twice about it. Even though my heart was in the right place, I always felt bad about being sneaky.

No Blow!

My Aunt Mary returned from her honeymoon and stopped by our house in Brandon, Manitoba, to visit our family.

Aunt Mary was very generous and bought a gift for each child in our family. My brother, Vince, who was 18 months old at the time, was given a wooden recorder whistle (the long ones that had the holes on the top). Since we lived in Brandon and my Aunt and her husband lived in Winnipeg, they spent the night at our place.

The next day, Vince came off the potty by himself and held up the whistle recorder to my Mom and said, "Mom, no blow!"

My mom responded by showing my brother how to use the whistle, until a very foul taste set in. She took the whistle and looked into the mouthpiece only to see poop smeared into it. Apparently, my brother thought that the toilet was the perfect playground for his new toy.

My mom was furious and embarrassed, and immediately broke the recorder over her knee and threw it in the garbage. All the while, the adults were laughing themselves to the point where they could barely breathe.

A couple weeks later, my Uncle Ben and Aunt Helen travelled to Brandon to visit my family with another special gift for Vince. This time, they brought him a gift that could not be broken; a recorder whistle made of metal.

After this incident, my aunts would tease my mom by saying "Sue, does this taste like crap? You're the only one who'd really know!"

It took quite a bit of time, but eventually my mom found some humour in this story. When she would repeat it, you'd swear it happened only yesterday, as she would gag and start to cluck when it got to the poopy part!

My mom, however, is not the only one in the family who has experienced non-traditional cuisine. Look for Nancy's story!

Bubble Trouble

As mentioned previously, my family lived in Brandon, Manitoba, for a few years through the 1970's. During this time, my Uncle Ben and Aunt Helen, along with my Aunt Mary and her husband would make trips out to spend the weekend with us.

This particular visit took place over Halloween. After us kids came in from trick 'r treating, my mom told us that we were not allowed to have any of the individually wrapped bubble gum as it was bad for our teeth.

Assuming that full chocolate bars, bags of chips, hard and soft sugar and caramel candies are bad for our teeth too, she must have had an ulterior motive because the bubble gum was off limits and we were told to fork it over.

Mom had the bright idea that her and her sisters should wage a little competition and see who could chew more bubble gum at once. If you've ever had the popular, individual-wrapped bubble gum, you know the pieces are one-inch square and depending on the freshness, some pieces are harder than others. Softer pieces are much easier to chew. Back in the 70's, the pieces were also bigger than they are today.

One after one, my mom and her sisters starting shoving pieces of gum in their mouths.

My Aunt Helen had a respectable number of bubble gum in her jaws, with 10 pieces being chewed like cow cud, before starting to gag. The sisters thought she did very well.

Not to be outdone, my Aunt Mary managed to fit 12 pieces in her mouth! I can only imagine how charming that must have looked. So much for the chewing-with-your-mouth-closed rule that was always reinforced growing up.

Mom went into full-throttle competitive mode, cramming 18 pieces of bubble gum in her pie-hole winning the challenge by a landslide! Impressive!

Mom won the title of the biggest mouth amongst her siblings. Not sure if that was the title she wanted to have, but she'd thrown down that gauntlet and earned the title fair and square.

I'd Like to Buy a Vowel

Our brother, Vince, the youngest of the siblings, lived at home long after the rest of us kids moved out. During this time, he and Mom spent a lot of time together watching TV and playing cards. Looking back, he had the advantage, as he was the only sibling who got Mom and Dad all to himself. Mom and Vince were super close and Vince liked to play jokes on mom from time-to-time.

After Vince moved out on his own, he used to periodically drop by and watch Wheel of Fortune with Mom. Vince would keep Mom company when Dad worked late or was out of town on business.

One day, mom found the perfect opportunity to turn the tables on her youngest child. Vince had announced that he was going to drop by for a visit that day, so Mom watched the Wheel of Fortune show with the same puzzles an hour earlier, thereby knowing the answers to each puzzle.

Vince came by as promised and Mom was very excited to watch their favorite show together. She knew this was a perfect joke to play on Vince. After one letter would be revealed, Mom would solve the puzzle and Vince would be amazed. The entire show went on like this and he said that he had the smartest mom, *ever*. He couldn't believe that she could solve the puzzle so quickly!!

Mom couldn't hold back for very long and confessed that she had already seen the show and knew the answers. Vince was a good sport and admitted that he'd been pranked! "Good one, Mom… You got me!!"

Mom had to be careful after that, as Vince had already started to hatch a plot for payback. I'm not sure what he did in return, but you can guarantee Mom got served-up a dose in return sometime down the road.

Now I Lay Me Down to Sleep
(This prayer was taught to our Mom by her Mom, our Grandma Friesen)

When each great granddaughter was born, they received this poem in a beautiful box frame from our Mom, their great-grandmother:

Now I lay me down to sleep
14 Angels watch me sleep
Two to my right
Two to my left
Two to my head
Two to my feet
Two that shall cover me
Two that shall wake me
Two that shall look after me
In my beautiful dreams

AMEN!

Nancy:

THE ELDEST SIBLING (THE ANGEL)
These next few stories and poems are either about Nancy or written to Nancy

"GOTCH-A"!

My sister Nancy used to live in Calgary, Alberta. We planned a trip to see our other sister, June, who recently moved to Penticton, BC.

I flew out from Winnipeg to Calgary and from there, we started our road trip further west to the Okanagan Valley, located amidst the beautiful Rocky Mountains in the interior of British Columbia.

The drive was beautiful and the scenery picturesque. The only drawback was the darn rain that wouldn't let up. It poured so hard at times our only refuge was the covered highway passes built into the side of the mountains.

We stopped in Golden, BC, for a quick bite to eat and some coffee in hopes that the rain would slow down, making the mountainous trek a little easier. The rain was coming down in buckets and I was going to look like a drowned rat if we tried to run across the packed parking lot without a jacket.

My jacket was buried somewhere inside my suitcase which was in the back of Nancy's car. Thankfully, I had packed my brand new windbreaker, which was 100% waterproof; perfect for the weather that we were getting.

Nancy raised the hatchback while I frantically was searching for my new windbreaker in my suitcase. The problem was that we had our suitcases stacked on top of each other, and I was unable to properly open my suitcase. Instead, I unzipped it partway and felt around for my jacket, all the while trying to duck and cover under the hatchback so I wouldn't get soaked.

"Ah ha!" I said, as my fingers found the type of material it was searching for. I pulled it out, put it on as quickly as I could and ran inside the coffee shop.

The line was long and after a short time we both needed to pee really badly. We left the line and headed to the ladies room. The washrooms were separated by a single door, which takes you in another corridor where individual men and women washrooms can be accessed. Both washrooms were occupied and there was another long line for the facilities. As patient Canadians, we waited and did the "pee-pee dance", shifting from side to side.

After a few minutes, Nancy asks me, "What's that?"

"What's what?" I replied.

She pointed at my leg and very calmly said, "That...hanging from your jacket?"

I looked down and within a half of a millisecond, ripped off the item which was stuck to the Velcro® closure of my jacket and shoved it in my pocket. Then I started to laugh. Nancy had no idea what I was laughing at, but I was out of control, which made everyone in line laugh. They had no clue what they were laughing at either – or maybe they did!

Finally, someone let me cut in line and use the washroom where I sat on the toilet and laughed very hard. Nancy, now using the men's washroom, could hear me and was laughing all by herself too, still not knowing what was so funny.

When I finally composed myself in the washroom, I had no make-up left and it looked like I had been crying for a day with a blotchy face and swollen lips.

Nancy met me in the bathroom corridor afterwards and asked me what was so funny. I started to giggle again as I squeaked out my response.

"It's a pair of underwear. Not just any underwear, either. It's my GIANT underwear! You know the ones that start at your upper thigh and go right up under your boobs," I replied.

We both laughed hysterically again as she told me that she thought it was a tuque that came with the jacket.

The server in the coffee shop told us that they could hear the commotion from inside the restaurant and wanted to be a part of the fun happening in the washroom area.

We had the giggles in the line-up and made total fools of ourselves, but what the heck? The mantra I live by is, "Hey... I'll never see these people again!"

And so the infamous travelling sisters started their adventure in <u>Derksen-style!!</u>

I'm Speeding Because I Have To Poop!

After Announcing Her Breast Cancer Diagnosis
(Written by June)

Roses are red
Violets are blue
You're a real fighter
We know that is true

This disease they call cancer
Has taken part of your breast
But can't take your spirit
Although it's one hell of a test

Your family will rally
And so will your friends
We will love you and support you
Until your mind and body mends

We won't forget about Jim
He is a very important part
The most loving generous man
With a very kind heart

Please remember to call
When you need a lift
We may be miles apart
But our love and support is our gift

Shawna J Peterson

On First Day of Chemotherapy
(Written by June)

Good morning sweet Nancy
Good morning to you
Look out the window
Is the sun is shining through?

It's a very big day
As the doctor you'll see
I just know he'll say yes
To start chemotherapy

Off to the races
Your treatment will start
One day closer to recovery
And that's the best part

With Jim by your side
Keeping you strong
And mom's spirit in the room
Things cannot go wrong

I love you and miss you
Plan on seeing you soon
Then we'll drive down the highway
And I'll hang someone a moon

Surviving Cancer Treatments
(Written by Shawna)

A journey that started
In summer last year
Has taken a toll
Of anxiety and fear

Breast cancer is nasty
There is no doubt
So many doc appointments
But you did not pout

With chemo first
And radiation to follow
You held your head high
Even when you felt hollow

With your spirit in tact
And faith you did cling
This disease hadn't a chance
Against God, our King

You're road to good health
Is well on its way
We're so happy you are winning
And will be here to stay!

Just Eat It!

Mom was petrified of mice. I think that her fear came from living on the farm with countless number of mice inside the home and endless amounts outside.

One morning when we lived on Alder Bay in Winnipeg, Dad had left for work and breakfast that day was cold cereal, not the usual porridge. The cereal was on the counter with the milk. Nancy, my oldest sister, started to eat the cereal and told mom she thought the milk was sour and that her cold cereal was burnt. Mom assured Nancy the milk was not sour and the cereal was fine. In the usual morning flurry of activity trying to get 4 kids fed and off to school, Mom told Nancy to, "just eat it!"

Mom had a nose that could seek out "sour" anywhere and anytime. If food even remotely smelled different, *out it went!* I'm a chip off the old block, in that respect. Cereal, however, is an entirely different story, because my mom never ate a bowl of cereal in her entire life. Of course, Nancy being the most obedient of us kids did what she was told and ate it.

A few minutes later mom opened the cupboard door under the sink to put something into the garbage and she saw a mouse scurrying through the cupboard.

Mom screamed at the top of her lungs, grabbed a chair and stood on it. While she continued to freak out, she managed to gain enough composure to call dad and ask that he come home to deal with the mouse.

Again, Nancy followed Mom's hysterical instructions by locking the mouse in the cupboard using jar rings around the handles. Keep in mind that we lived in Charleswood and my Dad worked a good 30-minute drive away in the Inkster Industrial Park area.

Dad turned around after just arriving at work, returned to the house, and promptly caught the mouse. At this point, Mom was standing on the piano bench in the living room until the mouse had met its demise.

Once mom settled down, she proceeded to clean out all the lower cupboards. There she discovered a hole in the cereal box. The so-called <u>burnt</u> cereal that Nancy ate for breakfast, were in fact mouse droppings.

For the life of me, I can't recall what the rest of us ate that morning but we know it wasn't that brand of cold cereal, or this story would have been more memorable for all of us kids.

Not many families can say that not only one, but also two members of their family have eaten turds. Is this family weird or what? I wouldn't want it any other way!! More weird stories to come!

Shawna J Peterson

Thank You
(Written by June)

Thank you so much
Nancy and Jim
For your great hospitality
And those wonderful evening swims

Your food is amazing
Your wine is the best
But eating 'green' cookies
Put my arms and legs to the test

Walks by the lake
Moose tracks on a cone
So relaxing and fun
Were we really ready to come home???

Thank you again
We love you so much
But next time please remember
To serve baking without that 'special' touch!!!

I'm Speeding Because I Have To Poop!

Jim's 60th Birthday
(Written by Shawna)

Happy birthday to Jim
Happy birthday to you
You can't be 60 yet
When you're so full of youth

You're almost retired
But do not despair
There's renos to do
Try not to pull out your hair

The upstairs, the downstairs
The house and the yard
Don't forget it's also time
To replace your ole car (dad really wants it)

So just because you're 60
That doesn't mean a thing
You're still young at heart
And are "Queen Nancy's" bestest King!

Shawna J Peterson

Thank You
(Written by Shawna)

How can I thank you
For the awesome week here
I was supposed to be caring for you
Instead we drank some beer

I'm so glad you were feeling good
But now I feel bad
As dads visit is post-chemo
That was MY job to be had

Your meals are so dee-lish
Your company, de-vine
And meeting your Penticton friends
Who really love their wine

I hope your next few weeks
Are as good as they can be
With dad, then June's visit
And laughing so hard, you'll pee

I'm Speeding Because I Have To Poop!

Sibling Fun

Top Photo: Nancy, June, and Shawna
Middle Row: Siblings signature performance of "We Are The World"
Bottom Row: Nancy, June, and Shawna; Nancy, Vince, and June

June:

THE FIRST MIDDLE CHILD (THE TRAILBLAZER)

These stories and poems have either been written to June, about June or a personal experience of June's

50th Birthday

(Written by Shawna and Nancy)

There once was a girl name June
Who one day decided to hang a moon
On the #1 highway
She said, "I'll do this my way"
I believe it was shortly passed noon

Now her sisters were quick and wise
And without a word of a lie
With a camera handy
We clicked at her fanny
And said "Hey June...SURPRISE!"

Now the funny thing is
The picture is amiss
And absolutely nowhere to be found
So we did our best
To recreate the trip out west
And hung this moon (with a few extra pounds)

Happy 50th birthday sis!!

Look for the "Moon for June" story that goes with this poem

More 50th Birthday Poems:

(Written by Shawna)
Roses are red
Pansies are pink
Now that you're 50
May your farts no longer stink

(Written by niece, Jackie)
Roses are red
Violets are blue
It would not be your birthday
Without "blow up" boobs

(Written by Nancy)
Roses are withered
Violets are dead
If turning 50 depresses you
Think of chocolate and sex instead

Poop and Scoop!

Have you ever been to the doctor with an issue that you think you already have the diagnosis for? Then it turns out that the doctor asks you to do certain tests in order to obtain the medical diagnosis? And once you realize what the test is, you regret going to the doctor in the first place and you start to feel fine?

Or have you gone to the doctor as you reach a milestone birthday and he subjects you to tests you've never had to do before? You wonder, why now? Why ever? No, don't make me do that!

This story is mostly about June, but I want to add a little preamble before we get to her experience.

I was having lower back issues and my septic system seemed to be affected during bouts of the attacks. I made an appointment to see my doctor, thinking he would take a back X-ray and a lower abdominal X-ray to see what the problem was. No, not even close.

He asked me to do a poop smear test! You know the one I'm talking about! The kind of test where you poop in the toilet, scoop it out with a spatula resembling the size of a match, and then smear it onto a piece of cardboard! You're supposed to do this without getting crap on your fingers or hands.

Really? Who would make someone do that? Why can't I crap into a container and drop it off at the nearest lab like we do urine tests? Seriously, people! This is gross! For someone who appreciates toilet humour, this is going too far – even for me!

"I am NOT digging in the toilet and scooping out my crap! No way, José!" I said to Dave.

David emphatically replied, "You have to do it Shawna! Tell you what? You take the poop and I'll scoop it out and smear it on the cardboard for you!"

"Aw, you'd do that for me?" I exclaimed. "Wow! I've got the best husband in the world!"

So, I did and he did and then we mailed it in the lab only to find out that my poop was fine. Of course it was fine! Eventually the issue resolved itself and that was that!

Now onto June's story.

This is an actual text conversation that took place between June and I:

Day 1: 1:30pm

June: Now I understand why you get Dave to do your shit sample test. I have shit everywhere! My legs, my kitchen floor, bathroom floor and carpet in my bedroom! I stink and am too embarrassed to hang my shitty washcloth outside. I may throw it out. LOL

Shawna: Did you shit yourself again? Hee hee ☺

Earlier this summer, June had an incident after holding it too long.

June: No, I thought I was finished and as I was running around looking for a pen, shit fell out of my bum and down my leg and chunks dropped on the floor. I just texted Nancy with my shit story too!!

Shawna: This is one for my book. Details, I want details! Holey Crap that's funny!

June: I'll excuse the pun! Nancy said she has to do that test too. I think Dave should do all of ours!

Shawna: What did Barry say?

June: He had already left for his massage with Robyn so I will tell him later

Shawna: Dave's a good man for sure! I'm working on my book at the lake and making great progress!

June: Enjoy your peace and quiet. It will get your creative juices flowing.

Shawna: Sounds like your juices were flowing this morning! Or maybe it was chunky, not juicy! LOL

June: Both! Stinky and shitty me! LOL

Day 2: 9:30am

June: Did the second poop test today and because my shit kept sinking to the bottom of the toilet bowl, I put paper on the bathroom floor and shit on the floor. Much easier, I must say! LOL

Shawna: Haaaa Haaaa Haaaa! You actually crapped on the floor? Haaaa Haaaa!!!

Shawna: Why do you have to do a poop test? I think I missed that part in the texts yesterday. I thought you just crapped everywhere because you didn't realize you weren't finished. So you have to do the "poop and scoop" test?

June: Yes! Because I am over 50 and the test includes taking a sample for three consecutive days, then mailing it all to the lab for testing

Shawna: Well, I'm turning 50 soon, so Dave will be a busy boy!

Day 2: 3:15pm

Shawna: Teresa suggested you put plastic wrap loosely over the toilet seat. You could try using a coffee filter that you could hold and dump into. You may need a few of them for strength

Shawna: Can I put this in my book as a "June story"?

June: Sure

Day 3: 9:15am

Shawna: How did poop test #3 go this morning?

June: Perfect! I have my diploma in shit testing!

END OF TEXT CHAIN

Mother's Day
(Written by Robyn)

Roses are red
Violets are blue
Your "new house" looks great
But it's still missing something (I know that didn't rhyme; you're better at this than me)

Raz made lots of wine
Red, white…a whole whack
And now it will have a place
On your colorful new rack!!

Left to right (back row): Brad, Jarrod (skydiving), Jay, David, Eric, Matty, and Robyn
Left to right (front row): Halle, Jackie, Dad, Mom, Shawna, Nancy, June, and Barry
(Missing: Jim, Carolyn, Annika, Makayla, Jayden, and Jeanette)

Dad's 40th Birthday Challenge

When our dad turned 40, Mom put on a big birthday bash for him!

She cooked my dad's favourite meal and we all gorged ourselves on homemade noodle soup until we could barely move.

Mom invited our aunts, uncles, and cousins to celebrate this milestone birthday together.

Soon after people started to arrive, June told dad that she thought she could drink him under the table.

Mom and dad were against underage drinking and didn't ever serve us alcohol; therefore, my dad wasn't sure how June was planning to accomplish this. He accepted the challenge knowing full well that she was too young to drink too much. This would be the very first time that June drank in front of Mom and Dad.

June started off drinking rye and cola, matching Dad, drink for drink. June had never drunk rye before and they were going down smooth. So smooth that she flushed down 6 of them in a short period of time. She may have had a 7th, had my Aunt Mary not mixed a vodka and orange juice for her as well.

June reached her maximum alcohol capacity while sitting in the living room and became paralyzed. She couldn't move and that's when Dad said that she'd had enough and it was time for bed.

Since Nancy was still living at home, June and I were still sharing a room, as well as a bed. There were no bunk beds in our house, only a double bed for two middle sisters to share.

I was only 13 years old and fast asleep when my sister Nancy and cousin Virginia poured a very plastered June into our bed. I woke up from all the commotion June was causing. She was looped!

June couldn't keep still and kept doing flip-flops in attempts to stop the bed spins. She turned to me and indicated that she was going to be sick and before I could move, she threw up all over the bed and all over me!

Do you recall what we had for dinner that day? Homemade noodle soup!

She heaved and heaved and kept puking. The noodle soup just kept coming up and she hurled it everywhere. It was like an infestation of 3-inch worms all over the bed and on the floor.

Had I not jumped out of bed to get help, I would have up-chucked my noodle soup, too. This was disgusting!

At the command of my parents, Nancy and Virginia came downstairs to see what was going on. After they witnessed the aftermath of regurgitated pasta, they saw June lying in bed covered in noodle soup vomit.

We only had one tub in the house which was located upstairs where the party was taking place, but June needed to get cleaned up and the girls were delegated the job. Guests could use the downstairs bathroom if they had to.

Nancy and Virginia dragged June upstairs and sat her on the toilet while they got the water running in the shower. Once the water was at an appropriate temperature, they undressed June and tried standing her up in the shower by herself. When they asked June to lean against the wall while they were getting soap and shampoo, she leaned against the shower curtain instead and fell out of the bathtub.

While all this was going on, the bedroom and our bed needed to be cleaned up. The room stunk to high heaven and was covered in puke.

Once both June and our room got cleaned up, June passed out and woke up with a hangover she would never forget.

Dad woke her up earlier than usual and made June play Pin the Tail on the Donkey. If being blindfolded and hung-over wasn't enough, instead of having the donkey poster on the wall, he exchanged it for a bowl of peanut butter. When June went to place the tail on the wall, she stuck her hand in the bowl and almost started vomiting all over again. June didn't like the texture of peanut butter at the best of times.

37 years later and June has never drunk rye and coke since.

Rightfully so, Mom was choked with Dad for letting June drink so much. Maybe Dad and June both learned a lesson that day. Then again, maybe not!

Shawna J Peterson

52nd Birthday
(Written by Robyn)

Roses are red
Violets are blue
"Holey s*#t the bed"
You're turning 52

No one would know it though
Thanks to Arbonne
I've got a smokin' hot momma
That's also fun, loving and strong

I thought you could use a laugh
Since it's been a tough year
Now get on the deck
And drink a few beers

52nd Birthday
(Written by Shawna)

There lives a lady name June
Who turns 52 wayyy too soon
She's sexy and fine
And loves her red wine
Even if it's not quite noon

Chocolate and champagne are also a fav
With a splash of OJ too
With Barry beside her
She can still pull an "all-nighter"
Without getting a sore "foo foo"!

Vince:

THE BABY OF THE FAMILY
These poems and stories are either about Vince, written by Vince or written to him

Our brother, Vinnie
(1969 – 2010)

To My Parents With Love
(Written by Vince)

Some people say that my parents are
A very special couple they admire from afar
Through thick and thin they are always there
Lending an ear and showing they care

They've taught me well and morally so
To be kind to others, friend or foe!
I've been shown to be polite
And never but never resolve with a fight

Now they've helped me see their ways
Not all I agree with even to this day
Some views I had when I was a teen
Have now fazed out and are no longer keen

To be on your own living out West
You think of your parents, the absolute best
Those thoughts bring hope and tears of joy
And fond memories of me as a little boy

Parents seem to have a loving touch
They take so little yet give sooooo much
And now they their babe who now has grown
Misses his parents who lives so far from home

Help – My Eyes Are Stuck!

As noted in a previous story, my brother, Vince, was a jokester! Whether making a crank call to Mom or doing goofy things to other friends and family, Vince was the person in our family that you had to watch (in a good way)!

I'm Speeding Because I Have To Poop!

Vince and I attended a local community carnival in the Charleswood area. Like me, Vince *loved* rides so we were a perfect pair to hit the annual exhibitions when they came to town.

Vince and I were on a ride, whereby you are in a cage sitting across from one another. The cage spins upside down, as it's rotating on a big Ferris wheel. As the ride stopped to let people on or off, our cage ended up at the very top of the Ferris wheel. The cage was in an odd position whereby I was laying on my back and Vince was suspended above me, looking down at me.

I looked at his face and his eyes went all screwy; one went one way and one went the other way, and he said to me, "Shawna, I think something is wrong with my eyes!"

I said, "You mean you can't look straight at me?"

"No, I think they're stuck like this!" he replied.

I started to panic and yell down to get help. Probably thinking that we were going to throw up all over everyone, the ride operator fast-tracked us down and let us off the ride.

Once we were out of the cage, Vince put his eyes back to normal and started laughing himself silly. It was only then that I knew he just pulled a fast one on his sister and I had fell for it hook, line, and sinker.

We laughed about that the entire day and in the many years that followed. I miss him and his pranks!

Left to right: Shawna, June, Vince, and Mom

Shawna J Peterson

In Honour of Our Brother, Vince's 1st Year Passing Anniversary

It's hard to believe
That one-year ago
Our telephone rang
And delivered a blow

A son, brother, uncle, husband,
Step-dad, grandpa and friend
A 41-year-old life
Came to an abrupt end

Your heart gave you troubles
And your mind became weak
Your just weren't strong enough
Even though God you did seek

In your darkest moments you know
That we never gave up hope
That you'd find your way back
And continue to cope

Even though your life may not have been
Exactly as it seemed
Before you left us
Your soul was redeemed

So dear son, brother,
Uncle and friend
God bless you and keep you
Until we see you again

Nephews:
Matthew and Jarrod

TRUE BLUE "BREW"
Being an avid football fan and wanting to connect with my nephew Matthew in his early teenage years, I asked him if he was interested in coming to a local football game with me.

After a quick consultation with my sister, it was agreed that I would pick Matty up and we would spend the evening together watching live football.

Everything went according to plan. I picked Matty up and we headed to the stadium for a fun evening of shouting at the top of our lungs while cheering on the "Big Blue".

Did I mention that I was young and foolish in my early adulthood? No? Well, this was one of the times where I demonstrated that very clearly.

During the first quarter, I had a temporary lapse in judgment and asked Matty if he wanted a beer. After all, I was there to supervise him and would ensure nothing would happen. Just one beer wouldn't affect him, right?

Although he told me that he never tasted beer before and was a little bit nervous since his parents weren't around, I assured him that it would be our little secret and a memory that we would share later in life with the family.

I could just imagine us years later around a campfire and Matty blurting out, "Mom, remember the football game that Aunty Shawna took me to when I was 13? Well, she bought me my very first beer, too!"

The shock and awe would have worn off quickly and we all would have laughed about it.

Yes, indeed, I was young and foolish... definitely not thinking of the consequences at the time!!

He chugged back the beer in a short period of time and sat very silent. I wasn't too concerned about him, as he seemed to handle the light beer pretty well.

I bought a second one for me and asked if he wanted to share it. He declined and said that he had started to feel a little fuzzy. I quickly realized that he needed some food and a hot chocolate or pop instead. There was no way that I could return him home with an upset tummy or walking a little sideways.

I put my adult-head on straight and behaved like an Aunty should for the rest of the game.

As I drove Matthew home, I thought about our agreement in keeping this secret from my sister. While I didn't tell Matthew that I was going to inform his folks on every detail of our evening, I think he knew.

When we arrived at his house, Matty headed straight to his room and barely acknowledged his parents.

Nancy looked at me strangely and asked how the evening went. I had to fess-up, right then and there. "Well, I have to tell you something that you're probably going to be upset about," I said. As I explained to both Nancy and her husband what I had done, they were speechless!

"I don't know what I'm more shocked at, Shawna. The fact that you bought him a beer at the age of 13 or that he actually drank the whole thing," Nancy exclaimed!

"Well, I'm very disappointed in you Shawna. I thought you would make better decisions than this," added my brother-in-law.

The ironic part of his speech was that he made many inappropriate remarks and decisions all the time and was calling *me* out! Well, I guess he had a right to, given the fact that this was his son he trusted in my care.

I asked that they go easy on Matty as it was completely my fault and I took 100% responsibility. Matty was in my care and I blew it!

I'm Speeding Because I Have To Poop!

Thankfully, after that episode, I was still able to spend time with Matty and niece, Jackie until they relocated to Calgary in 2000.

Matty and I can share that story now and chalk it up to an Aunty trying to be cool. Yep! Definitely a bad decision but Matty, indeed, will always remember who bought him his first beer!

For Matty's 32nd birthday, I wrote him this little poem on Facebook:

> Happy Birthday Matty
> Happy Birthday to You
> Do you remember when you were 13
> And I bought you your first brew?

That posting resulted in Matty's uncle giving me the "<u>what-for</u>" again!

Nephew Matty's 31st Birthday
(Written by Shawna)

Happy birthday nephew
Happy birthday Matt
Now that you're over 30
So have a real good "shat"

Hey, I never promised you beautiful poetry in this book...just real ones

Nephew and Niece, Jarrod and Robyn Tymm

I'm Speeding Because I Have To Poop!

Jarrod's 30thst Birthday
(Written by June – his Mom)

Happy Birthday Dear Jarrod
Happy Birthday dear son
This is the year
For you to have fun

Your meniscus is out
Your knee in good shape
To jump out of planes
Without even a scrape

No more saunas to sell
Or sales pitches to spew
Take all of your money
Make your dreams come true

Get in all those dives
We'll jump tandem, you'll see
I'll wear some old clothes
Because surely I'll pee

All kidding aside
I'm so proud of you
You've stuck to your plan
And will love what you do

And speaking of love
One day really soon
You'll meet a young lady
Who'll send you to the moon

But for now you must celebrate
Your 30th birthday
We'll be there in spirit
Even though we're far away!!

Nephew Matty Luff with wife Carolyn, and children, Annika, Makayla, Jayden, and Jeanette

Niece: Jackie (And Jay)

JACKIE'S SURPRISE SHOWER

Whenever my niece Jackie would start to date someone, we would count the number of monthly cycles that each boyfriend would get through, in order to determine the seriousness of each relationship. Any boyfriend that made it past 3 monthly cycles had the patience of Job and was considered a contender for long-term status.

When Jackie and Jay started to date, everyone hoped and prayed that he would make it through each monthly cycle. Month after month, our prayers were answered.

"Yes! They made it through another one!" we would say to each other.

When Jackie and Jay announced their engagement, we knew this was <u>the one</u> for Jackie. She was going to become Mrs. Jackie Kennedy! Yes, Jay's last name was Kennedy!

Everyone loved Jay and he seemed to fit in perfectly with this wacky family. He met the approval of Jackie's cousin Robyn. Jackie and Robyn were always very close growing up and even when they lived in different cities, they kept in touch on a regular basis.

My cousin Pearl planned a wedding shower for Jackie, which took place in Calgary, Alberta. Pearl asked me if I would fly to Calgary to participate in the shower by doing a presentation on intimacy-enhancing products, which I sold at the time.

"Of course, I will. It's an honour and privilege to be a part of Jackie's celebration and I wouldn't miss it for the world," I replied.

I flew out a couple days before the wedding shower to visit my sister Nancy. During this time, we kept a very low profile and avoided the phone in order to keep my visit a secret from Jackie.

The day of the shower, Jackie's Maid of Honour and Bridesmaids came to Nancy's house to decorate. Pearl, Nancy, and the girls were busy preparing the house and getting the trays of food and beverages ready while I set up the product table for the presentation.

When Jackie pulled up, everyone avoided the living room window area to prevent Jackie from seeing in. I, in the meantime, was upstairs waiting for the right time to make my appearance and give Jackie yet another surprise!

When she walked through the front door, she quickly knew that this was going to be a party in her honour.

From upstairs, I heard, "Oooooh, we're having one of <u>those</u> parties!! Yeah!!! I can get stocked up for our honeymoon," Jackie exclaimed.

One of Jackie's friends, who was present at the shower used to sell Passion Parties products as well, therefore Jackie just assumed that she would be doing the presentation.

I slowly crept down the stairs, came up behind Jackie, covered her eyes and said "Surprise!"

She turned around and screamed at a decibel that can only be reached by professional opera singers, "Aunty Shawna, you're here!! Are you doing the Passion Parties presentation?"

After confirming her suspicion, I also informed her that any credits that would usually go to the party hostess, would be given to her. With 15 ladies in the group, she was likely to have some very good honeymoon products.

Instead of buying traditional gifts, the ladies also donated Bridal Bucks towards Jackie's purchases.

While I cannot recall the exact amount of credits and Bridal Bucks Jackie received, I remember that she walked away with a lot of expensive products at no cost to her. Indeed, this would be a honeymoon to remember!

I was thrilled to be included at Jackie's celebration and was grateful that my cousin Pearl suggested it; so was Jackie, I believe!

JAY's 40th Birthday
(Written by Shawna)

There lives a young man named Jay
Who said "I'm 40…what the hay?"
I've got a hot broad
Who has an amazingly sizzling bod
This is going to be one amazing day!!!

Now turning 40 isn't so bad
In fact, it can be kind of rad
They are better than the 30's
And exceedingly better than the 20's
Plus your one smokin' hot dad

So on your 40th birthday
Let me take this time to say
Pay no attention to your age
But its time to turn that 30 "something" page
With Jackie giving you a celebratory day

Happy birthday Big Guy!!

Jackie and Jay

Niece: Robyn (And Brad)

YOUR WAY
In Honor of Robyn's Graduation (June 25, 2004)
(Words Changed by Shawna)

VERSES:
And…now the time is near
You celebrate…your graduation
Robyn Dear…it's all so clear
Time for rest…and relaxation

The friends… you've met at school
Are so cute…. and very cool
Be proud….. and take a bow
You did it your way
Regrets…We've all had a few
Wish I'd spent ….More time with you
And now….You're all grown up
Oh my oh my…But how the time flew

I look…At you tonight
With pride and joy…And I must sa-ay
You worked hard…With much regard
You did it yourrrrrrr way

BRIDGE:
Mexico bound….You had a blast
And now you're saving….You money fast
You're a-a-aamigo…Is somewhere there
Standing innnnn……a g-string underwear
They're all so cute….You had a hoot
You did it your way

VERSE:
Post Mexico….Yes, there were boys
First Billy Bob…..Lisandro recent
But your freedom rings….Independence sings
Or you'll end up…. Naked and indecent

Hang on….To your roots
Cuz they may want….To spend your loot
You've raised the bar….It's who you are
You did it yourrrrrr way

Professor

I used to sell intimacy-enhancing products for Passion Parties, and loved it.

The products consist of romantic and pamper-yourself items as well as a playful line.

When people hear about these types of products, they automatically think only of the playful line. While that's perfectly natural, most folks don't realize that there is much more to this company than just the toys.

My main motivation was helping married couples stay together. In this disposable world where many couples treat their marriages like a broken electronic item and simply toss it away, I wanted to make a difference and help couples stay together in a unique way.

As a consultant, I heard a lot of personal information about my customers and was able to help struggling couples find that spark again by the use of lotions, creams, scented oils, candles, etc. At times, I knew that our products were not the solution to their marital issues and recommended counseling or spiritual guidance as an alternative.

Yes, of course there was the playful line too, but my passion was to help married couples stay together. These items were not meal replacements, so to speak, but rather a vitamin for long-term benefits.

Back to the real story

My mom and dad, sister June, niece Robyn, cousin Pearl, husband, Dave, and I, booked a trip to Cuba.

On our first evening in Cuba, several of us went to the beach bar to enjoy a mojito and watch the sunset. One of the security guards sat down to chat with us and took a liking to Robyn.

After explaining that we were from central Canada (which he didn't have a clue where that was), he asked what we all did for a living. One by one, we all went around the table and explained where we worked.

When it came around to me, I indicated that I had two jobs; the first was working in the public sector and the other being an independent consultant with Passion Parties. I explained my role with the feds as best I could and he somewhat understood; however, he did not comprehend the concept behind Passion Parties.

The language barrier was evident as I was trying to explain the different products I sold at home parties (lotions, candles, oils, creams… and toys).

He looked very perplexed and said, "What kind of toys?"

"The adult kind," I replied, while trying to think of a way out of this conversation.

He had no idea what I was talking about and I wasn't about to explain what and how these products worked.

Robyn took it upon herself to *tactfully* and fully clothed, demonstrate how one might use the item.

He jumped back, pointed directly at me and said, "Ah! You professor!!"

I'm sure what he meant was that I educated people; however, the way he translated it came out very comedic.

I haven't sold these products for a few years but the name has stuck and, to this day, Robyn still refers to me as "professor".

We're So Proud Of Her
Another Graduation Song for Robyn
To the Tune of "Saw Her Standing There"
(Words Changed by Shawna)

VERSE:
Well she was just 17
You know what I mean
Robyn graduates
From high school in the "Pe-eg"
She never lived in the city
OOOOOHHH
Until her final year

She started E--K
Made friends right away
Started hanging out with girl and boys alike
Language she learned by her buddies
OOOOOOHHH
In her fii-nal year

BRIDGE:
And her red rose-y cheeks
With her perrrr-fect teeth
And a set of boobs to be envie-e-e-d

VERSE:
She's a joy to be around
Very seldom is she down
She is sweet and kind
And give you all she can

She's loved as she loves
Like no other
OOOOOHHHH
And we're so proud of her

"I Do"

When my niece Robyn and her fiancé, Brad, asked me to be their marriage commissioner for their special day, I was so pleased.

I had put the bug in their ear a year earlier when our friend's daughter got married and her aunt (Pat, who you will read about later in this book) performed the ceremony.

I honestly had no idea they would seriously consider this and felt very privileged to perform this duty for such an important occasion.

I completed my application for a temporary Marriage Commissioner license and started to work on the ceremony.

I researched other Marriage Commissioners websites and quickly became educated on the various pieces of information that are required or typically included in marriage ceremonies. I also thought long and hard about the advice I would give my daughter (if I had one) about marriage, commitment, love, acceptance, forgiveness, and all that goes along with spending your life with someone. I also reflected on a conversation I had with my colleague Vaughn regarding the difference between like and love and included that as a part of the ceremony message. I asked permission to include a marriage blessing from God and was thrilled when they put their stamp of approval on it.

I prepared the draft service and met with Robyn and Brad to review. After some minor changes, the ceremony messaging and service was complete.

The end result was a lovely 15-minute wedding ceremony on May 31, 2014, that I was so proud and honoured to be a part of.

Thank you, Robyn and Brad, for including me on one of the most important days of your life.

I'm Speeding Because I Have To Poop!

Robyn and Brad on their Wedding Day, May 31, 2014

Chapter II

Becoming a Peterson

Shawna and Dave tied the knot on April 22, 1994 in Las Vegas, Nevada

Here Comes the Bride

Dave and I talked about buying a different house as we were outgrowing the small St. Boniface home that we spent almost 4 years in. This home had special meaning to Dave, as his dad was raised in it and family weekends and holidays were spent there with his Nana. Dave purchased the home from his Nana in the mid 1980's and it suited his needs quite well.

In 1990, I moved in with Dave and shortly thereafter, we bought a golden retriever, Lucas. A few years later, with Dave's son Eric almost 9 years old, it was apparent that we were outgrowing the house.

At the same time, I suddenly felt this urge to be married. Dave and I discussed this without pressure and mulled over options.

Dave and I have never had a traditional relationship so it stood to reason that our engagement would be much the same.

The big wedding proposal from Dave took place while waking up from an afternoon nap and went something like this.

"So, do you want to buy a different house or do you want to get married? Your choice."

I was in awe with the romance involved in the delivery of his proposal. Of course, I chose marriage over the house and the wedding plans began.

After considering many plans (including a double wedding with his brother, Harvey), a Las Vegas wedding on April 22, 1994, was set with a reception in early May in Winnipeg for family and friends.

"Nobody's invited but everybody's welcome," was our message to family and friends.

We didn't want to put pressure on anyone, as destination weddings were expensive back then. It turns out we had quite a crowd.

We showed up at the airport and someone snuck up behind me, put their hands over my eyes and said, "Guess who?"

I knew exactly who it was! My buddy Craig Crompton who was also a former roommate had come to see me off. I turned around and gave him a big hug after which he proceeded to introduce me to his female friend.

I recognized her immediately, but couldn't remember her name or where I knew her. I think her name was Laura. It turns out we went to high school in Winnipeg together; however, Craig had met her while living in Calgary! Talk about a small world!

Craig and I had lost touch over the past few years and, last I knew, he lived in Calgary, Alberta. I just assumed he moved back to Winnipeg and was at the airport to see me off.

"I heard there was a wedding in Las Vegas that I simply could not miss," he said.

My jaw dropped! He in fact, still lived in Calgary and had flown to Winnipeg so that he could travel with the entire wedding group. How awesome was that? Pretty darn awesome!!

My sister Nancy tossed back a few Brown Cows, as she wasn't a good air traveler at the time. Oh, how things have changed! She now travels all over the world with no libation required!

On the plane, the flight crew was instructed to give our wedding party free drinks, but since we were scattered all over the plane, they had a hard time keeping track. My brothers-in-law at the time (who are no longer my brothers-in-law), made sure their flight attendant knew they were with our party and took full advantage of an open bar. The plane ride was loud and fun. We were only a group of 16 but we sounded like there were 50 of us.

We arrived in Las Vegas mid-afternoon and had the rest of the day to finalize the wedding plans; however, since the courthouse was already closed, we waited until the next morning to obtain our marriage certificate.

We woke up in the morning and with both our parents in tow, David and I headed to the County Courthouse where we got legally married.

We completed our marriage application with a small golf pencil, then stood in line and waited our turn until our number was called. A magistrate explained the legalities and typed up our wedding certificate on an IBM Selectric typewriter (the younger generation will not know what that antiquated equipment is). We each signed the wedding certificate and were legally married.

The ceremony took place at 4pm on April 22, 1994, in a small chapel called *The Little Church of the West*. The quaint chapel that held approximately 30 people was the perfect venue for our nuptials!

As Dave stood at the front of the church, I hid outside behind the church door and waited for the music to cue me in.

All of the sudden, our friend Barry and his wife (now ex-wife), came whipping around the corner of the church. In front of an open church door, Barry enthusiastically says, "Hey Shawna, how the hell are ya?"

All eyes in the church turned to him and he realized that he had walked in just as I was about to start down the aisle. They quickly took their seats and the ceremony began.

The pastor gave a short message. Our witnesses, Johnny Gordon and Teresa Dyck, signed the marriage certificate and within 15 minutes, we were pronounced husband and wife. After a short photo shoot, it was time for the celebration to begin.

We adjourned to the pool area where guests took pictures while sipping on long-island iced teas.

One picture included my dad balancing himself on a pair of roller skates. When Dave and I announced our engagement, I asked my dad if he would walk me down the aisle. Dad, who never cries, had a tear in his eye when he accepted. Trying to break this awkward moment, I said, "Dad, I'll walk fast and put you in a pair of roller skates so you can keep up with me." We hauled those roller skates from Winnipeg to Vegas and made sure we captured the moment (No, he didn't wear them in the church).

We purchased bottles of champagne for each of our guests, which were placed inside each hotel room while we enjoyed a feast at the seafood buffet. The complimentary wine bar was taken full advantage of by everyone. In fact when dinner was over and the wine bar was dry, my dad attempted to take the easy way out of the restaurant area and scaled over the thick red velvet rope that sectioned off the restaurant. With one leg on the restaurant side of the rope and the other on the casino side, he fell. Not only did my dad go down, so did a series of pylons. Yep, right on his arse as we watched the roped pylons fall one after the other, much like a set of dominos.

My mom, embarrassed and shaking her head, stepped over him and said, "I'm going to the casino. Get off the floor," and kept walking.

I'm Speeding Because I Have To Poop!

Everyone went back to their hotel rooms, changed clothes, grabbed their bottles of chilled champagne, and met up at the pool area where we continued to celebrate.

Things got a little carried away when a couple of the guests (names are omitted to protect the guilty) stripped down to their undergarments and jumped in the pool, which was closed for the night. Security guards became involved and we were evicted from the pool area, but not before my sister, Nancy peed her pants on the grass.

After that, everyone scattered in different directions. The honeymoon had started. We told everyone to have a good vacation and we would see them in the lobby on departure day.

We walked The Strip from end to end and experienced Freemont Street in Old Vegas, located in the downtown area.

With the exception of the group bus tour to the Hoover Dam, we only saw our friends and family when we would bump into them on The Strip or in a restaurant at our hotel.

While on the Hoover Dam tour, the tour operator offered us a half-price special on the Grand Canyon air only tour for the following day. Our time was limited as we were returning home the same day as the Grand Canyon tour; however, since we had a late flight back to Winnipeg, there was time to squeeze this in.

We originally booked an air-only tour. When we arrived at the airport, they gave us the deluxe air and ground tour for the same price. Keep in mind that we only paid half-price for the air-only tour. Therefore, we considered this a deal we could not pass up. The only issue was that we were under a time constraint, as we needed to be checked out of our hotel by 3pm and the deluxe tour wasn't going to return us until closer to 5pm. Since our ground transportation from the hotel to the airport was only picking us up at 7pm, we knew we wouldn't miss our flight home by taking advantage of this rare opportunity.

We called the hotel, explained our situation and made arrangements for them to pack our suitcases. They let our parents access our room to assist and supervise, then held our bags at the concierge area till we arrived. After running a little late, we arrived at the hotel by 6pm and met up with our group in the lobby.

My mom, being the lucky person she's always been, plunked her final 75 cents in a slot machine at the airport and won $125 US. In fact, my mom and dad were both lucky and won enough to pay for their entire holiday in Vegas!

The reception in Winnipeg was so much fun! We celebrated with all of our friends and family who weren't able to make it to Las Vegas.

P.S. We were married in Las Vegas on April 22, 1994, and moved into our new home on April 28, 1994. Who says you can't have it all? I got the proposal, wedding AND the house! He got "me"!

I'm Speeding Because I Have To Poop!

Dad and Shawna in Las Vegas

Shawna J Peterson

Meet My Hunky Husband, Dave

Potato Salad Special

I had just received good news at work so Dave and I celebrated by going to the local watering hole for a bud, spud, and steak night. Since we lived so close to the hotel, we walked over instead of driving.

After a great meal and a couple of beers, Dave and I headed home to start preparations for company who were coming for lunch the next day. I was making my mom's famous potato salad!

On the way home, we acted like goofy newlyweds and Dave pretended to carry me over a threshold in someone's backyard. It was actually a red plastic snow fence, but we pretended it was a threshold. In his attempts to lift me over, he darn near sent both of us arse-over-tea-kettle. The fence was high and the snow was deep, which made it hard to scale over the fence with me in his arms.

As we cut through people's yards to get home quicker, Dave stopped and decided that this was a fabulous time to act like a 6 month old puppy and proceeded to water the tires on an expensive vehicle sitting in someone's driveway. We laughed all the way home and continued being total goofballs.

When we finally arrived home, exhausted from laughing and trenching through the snow, it was time to get to work on the potato salad. The ritual in our family was to boil the potatoes and eggs the night before, let them cool in the fridge overnight, then put the salad together the next day. We put the potatoes and eggs in separate pots and turned the elements onto medium-high to boil. In the meantime, what *were* we going to do?

Since we were already on a roll, we continued our charade as newlyweds and got frisky. We knew we had about 25 to 35 minutes until the eggs and potatoes would be done, leaving us lots of time to have fun.

Our fun must have been a gallop instead of a canter, as we fell into a deep sleep before the potatoes and eggs were done and did not hear the stove timers go off. I woke up smelling something strange and when I opened my eyes, our main floor in our tiny St. Boniface home was filled with smoke.

After screaming at Dave to wake up, we leapt out of bed and headed straight to the kitchen, where our golden retriever, Lucas, was enjoying the spuds that were now all over the kitchen floor. We turned off the elements, threw the pots out the back door into a snow bank, opened every window and door in the house and waited for the smoke to clear.

February is bitterly cold in Winnipeg and we had just woken up naked from a dead-sleep in a smoke-filled house. Needless to say, we flung a few clothes on and retreated outside until it was safe to re-enter the house.

While outside, we inspected the cook wear which was completely ruined. The bottoms of the pots were black and the potato pot still had some charcoal potatoes stuck to the bottom of it. The pot with the eggs was empty!

When it was safe to return into to the house, we entered the kitchen and there were potatoes and eggs on the counter, on the stove, on the floor (the ones that Lucas hadn't yet eaten), on the tops of the cupboards and eggs… Oh my, the eggs were all over the ceiling. They had exploded everywhere! If you've ever had your house egged you know how hard it is get egg off a surface. This was a mess!

Dave and I still can't figure out how we didn't hear the noise of the exploding eggs and potatoes. Our bedroom was right beside the kitchen and the stove was beside our bedroom door for crying out loud!

Even though we were wide awake in the middle of the night – and stayed that way for a very long time – we decided against trying the potatoes and eggs again. Instead, we waited until morning and made the best potato salad we could, but it didn't taste the same! Can't mess with Mama's recipes!

55th Birthday
(Written by June)

Happy birthday dear Dave
Happy birthday to you
Your birthday's important
But hunting season is too

I wish safety and fun
With your buddies on the hunt
But I still hope you miss
Sorry… I must be blunt!

So have a good day
Have a rye and sit back
While Shawna has her way with you
And shags you in the sack!

The shining star and love of my life, David

Eric:
MY SECOND FAVORITE PETERSON GUY

The Peterson Family: Dave, Shawna and Eric

I started dating Dave, Eric's dad shortly before Eric turned 4 years old. He's now almost 30, so picking out one or two memorable experiences is next to impossible. Instead, I've decided to share a collection of memories that still put a smile on my face when recalling Eric's younger years with us.

Eric was always a very social kid. He loved to get together with his cousins from the Derksen side (Matthew and Jarrod in particular), his Grandma and Grandpa Peterson, as well as Nana and Papa (my folks).

Early Saturday mornings often consisted of watching a few cartoons, having a bowl of cereal, then heading to my folks place for coffee and a visit. Dave enjoyed sleeping in on weekends, so Eric and I would head out on our own.

My dad *loved* joking around with Eric. At first, his reactions to my dad's jestering were a little stiff and standoffish, however it didn't take long and Eric would be egging my dad on to initiate a tease.

Some grandparents want to see but not hear their grandchildren. Not my folks! When they had an opportunity to spend time with them, they were down on the floor with Lego, building little things with a toy tool set, coloring or playing Lite Bright.

As the kids got older, the grandchildren learned to play cards with Nana, the shark! She was a ruthless card player and loved to win. I'm sure she threw a few games to appease the grandkids every now and again.

Yes, Eric and I loved these Saturday or Sunday mornings with my folks, especially if Jarrod or Matthew were visiting as well. I was thrilled to spend time with Eric as it brought out my inner-child and I was able to live life through the eyes of a young boy. While Dave was anxious for Eric to be old enough to go hunting, fishing and do all the manly things that guys do, I loved taking him to movies, go carting, and water-sliding at Fun Mountain. Another favorite past time was to visit my sister Nancy, who had a big pool in her back yard. Eric and his cousins would play for hours, exhausting themselves silly.

If Dave was on-call and wasn't able to plan much, Eric and I would entertain ourselves and play mini-golf or hit Tinker Town for an afternoon of rides and candy floss. As he got older, we kicked it up a notch and enjoyed the thrill rides at the Red River Exhibition grounds near Polo Park. Of course, we also attended the occasional Winnipeg Blue Bomber football game together. I had so much fun with him and treasured those times together.

By now you may have realized that Eric did not live with us full-time. We cherished the scheduled weekends he spent with us immensely and were extremely appreciative of any additional time that was available.

As Eric got older, he was able to travel with us. We took a road trip out to Alberta where we enjoyed an incredible day at the West Edmonton Mall. Between the thrill rides and waterpark, we wanted to experience as much as we could with Eric.

On this same vacation, Dave's aunts, uncles, and cousins were able to finally meet him at the Mann Family Reunion, which took place in Sylvan Lake, Alberta. While a little shy, he still made friends with other second cousins his age and enjoyed swimming, horseback riding, and campfires with them. Eric had never been this far from home before and was a little apprehensive sleeping in a strange place and meeting 30 or more new relatives from his Dad's side. However, his good nature and social skills kicked in which made it easier for him to adjust.

Since the Mann Family Reunion traditionally took place over the September long-weekend, Eric needed to quickly return home in order to start school. While our road trip continued, we put him on a plane from Calgary where his mom met him at the Winnipeg Airport to conclude his summer vacation. This was Eric's first experience on an airplane and he did great!

On another occasion, Dave and I planned a trip to Calgary to visit my sister and family, as well as his brother and wife for Christmas. After getting permission from Eric's mom, we were very excited that we could take this vacation together. Since we also wanted to participate in the Christmas festivities at home, Eric celebrated with his mom's side on Christmas Eve, as did we, with Dave's side of the family. After an early lunch on Christmas Day with the Derksen side, Dave, Eric, and I boarded a plane to continue the celebration with other family members in Calgary. The trip was fun and Eric was able to spend more time with his cousin Matthew who he had missed after my sister and her family moved to Calgary. It was nice for Eric to have spent that Christmas with all sides of his family.

There were a few times when Dave would escort Eric to Boy Scout events and attended a father-son excursion, which tested outdoor abilities and endurance. I'm not certain how much fun Eric had, but Dave said it was good for character building.

Growing up, Eric was not athletic; however, he did find one sport that he became quite passionate about. Football became a full-time commitment and he was *fantastic* at it. He played Left Guard on the O-Line for the Transcona Nationals. While we made it out to many practices and games, often standing beside our car, under a tree or by the bleachers, we didn't see as many as we could have, which is a sad regret.

Unfortunately, we can't turn back the clock and recapture those days; however, as all parents would confess, "We did our very best at the time." We kept Eric connected with all sides of his extended family which paid-off as Eric has maintained his relationships with the Derksen and Peterson families to this day.

The time we spent with Eric will *always* be treasured. I loved him as a little boy, through the tough teenage years, and as much today as a full-grown man as I ever have! I feel incredibly blessed to have such an amazing stepson in my life!

I'm Speeding Because I Have To Poop!

Eric Adam Peterson

Shawna J Peterson

Eric's 29th Birthday
(Written by Shawna)

Happy birthday Eric
Happy 29th birthday to you
May you party hearty with your friends
And of course with Courtney too

It seems like just yesterday
When you were only 3
And we first met at the house
Of Auntie June and "ex" Tracy

Your smile won me over
Your giggle made me laugh
You obviously do the same for Courtney
As she's now your "other half"

So Eric let me say this
How proud I am of you
We couldn't ask for a better son
I know you're dad feels the same way too!

It's Great to be a Canadian, Eh?

During our stay at an all-inclusive resort in a remote Mexican fishing village, Dave and I checked out several bungalows for rent, as an alternative to all-inclusive holidaying. One particular bungalow stood out because of its unique features. I refer to it as a *Swiss Family Robinson* home, but it's officially called Las Cabana del Capitan. It's a 3 story external walk-up where 75% of your living space is outside under a clay tile roof. The lush walkways to each unit lead you to the patio, then into the living room and kitchen area. An entrance into the air-conditioned bedroom and bathroom area are located directly off the kitchen. The large pool, hot tub, and a super-sized palapa are surrounded by grass and a breath-taking view of the Pacific Ocean. We fell in love with this bungalow and decided that if we ever tried a bungalow-style holiday, this would be the place we would stay.

We finally decided to try this Swiss Family Robinson holiday and booked a 19-day vacation at Las Cabana del Capitan. We were so excited! A new adventure! Something we had never done before! This was going to be fantastic!!

As required for international travel, we arrived at the airport 3 hours ahead of time and were more than ready to start our vacation. The aircraft however had mechanical issues and we were grounded until the repairs were completed. Once the plane was fixed, they needed to get a new crew, which caused additional delays. Finally, we were up-up-and-away!

Unlike all-inclusive resorts that provide ground transportation between the airport and accommodations, we made arrangements with our bungalow for a driver to pick us up at the Puerto Vallarta (PV) airport.

We fully expected someone to be there, holding a sign with our names on it. As the crowd thinned, we realized that our ride had likely left without us as our plane was over an hour late and the driver gave up waiting. Now what? We talked to some taxi drivers who were willing to give us a ride until they knew how far they had to drive us at midnight.

They looked at us and said, "No, no, no... too far." Crap! Even the Taxi Coordinator tried to get taxi drivers to take us to Guayabitos, but nobody wanted to drive all that way through the Sierra Madre Mountains for a one-way fare. Eventually, we were the only ones left in the airport and the taxi coordinator said "Okay, I'll take you for $100 US."

Done and done! The deal was made! Had we of used the driver from the bungalow, it was only going to cost us $25 US, but we were hooped and had little choice.

Parched and tired, we stopped at a 24-hour convenience store to pick up a couple bottles of cola for the 75-minute road trip. We headed north, leaving Puerto Vallarta behind us and onto new adventures in our Swiss Family Robinson home for 19 glorious days! The trip had started off a little rough with plane delays and ground transportation issues; however, we were now on our way to paradise and ready for the next exciting event. Little did we know, it was only a short time later before that event would occur.

After getting lost a couple times in Guayabitos, the driver eventually found our bungalow. We paid the man, collected our luggage, thanked him profusely for going out of his way to get us to our destination, and waved goodbye to him as he drove back to Puerto Vallarta.

Approaching 1:30am and exhausted from the journey, we were still super pumped and couldn't wait to settle into our bungalow. We tried opening the gate which was locked. Hmmmm... our arrival was expected, so we were sure that someone would be here to let us in.

We knocked lightly and whispered, "Hello! It's the Peterson's. Is anyone there?"

We kept our voices low, as we didn't want to wake up any of the guests. Nothing! No answer! Now what? After a few more attempts, we gave up. It appeared that we were not going to be able to get into our bungalow and we had to come up with a plan B.

We did what any good, creative, and patient Canadian would do. We poured ourselves a drink on the sidewalk beside the bungalow gate and pondered our options. We had packed travel mugs and purchased duty free in Winnipeg; with the colas we picked up on route from the PV airport, we were set! We had munchies in our carry-on luggage, therefore we weren't going to starve or dehydrate anytime soon.

Our bungalow was located directly beside a walkway going from our street to the ocean. We borrowed a plastic resin table and chair set that were stacked up along the walkway and perched ourselves along the ocean wall. We pulled out a portable DVD player from our luggage, poured ourselves another drink, opened up a bag of munchies, and watched a movie as the waves lapped onto the beach.

A while later, a homeless man collecting recyclables wandered by and asked us, in exceptional English, what we were doing. We explained that we got locked out of our bungalow after our plane landed late and ride abandoned us. We were simply killing time until we could get into our bungalow next door. He told us that he knew the night watchman, and was surprised that no one answered our calls through the gate. He continued to walk down the beach collecting plastic and glass bottles.

An hour or so later, the same homeless man came running up to us and said, "He's up! He's up! Go see him now!"

Apparently the night watchman had fallen asleep and didn't hear our knocking or voices when we were dropped off at 1:30am. At 3am, we were finally able to access our bungalow.

By the time we unpacked all of our things, it was rounding 4am and the sun had peaked over the mountains. There was no point in going to bed, so we made ourselves a pot of coffee, threw in a splash of Irish Cream, and sat in the pool area by the ocean and watched the sunrise. It was a perfect start to an amazing holiday! Plans don't always have to go smoothly to be perfect! Canadians know how to turn lemons into lemonade! It's great to be a Canadian, eh?

Bear'ing It All

Holidays growing up meant camping in a trailer at West Hawk Lake, Manitoba, Detroit Lakes, Minnesota, or a road trip out west to visit friends and relatives.

As far back as I can remember, we always had either a soft-top or hardtop trailer. If we tented, I don't remember it. Summer camp meant sleeping in cabins or lodges, but not tents. It's not that I was opposed to tenting – I was simply not exposed to it.

Dave, on the other hand, is the ultimate outdoorsman. He grew up in Pinawa, Manitoba, and his playground was the vast wilderness only feet from his back door. He enjoyed the simple things in life. Canoeing to remote areas off the Winnipeg River system, pitching a tent, and cooking meals over an open fire. It's only natural that he would want me to experience these serene and peaceful places that he had come to love.

We set a weekend aside in early June and decided it was time for me to experience the paradise that Dave spoke of. I had absolutely no idea what backwoods camping meant or the adventure he would be taking me on. When I mentioned this outing to my folks, my mom planted a seed that gave me a little stir inside.

"My mom said that there are bears out there," I bluntly said to Dave. I got excited at the prospect of seeing one, but nervous at the idea of running into one. I wanted to see one all right, but only from a distance.

Dave responded by stating that he had been backwoods camping for years, had never seen a bear out there, and for me not to get my hopes up.

Dave borrowed his buddy's small fishing boat and motor which transported us and our gear from Caddy Lake to North Cross Lake, ending at a private campsite known to local folks as Rosie's Cabin. There used to be a cabin on the land, before it burnt down several years prior. The land became a part of the Whiteshell Provincial Park, open for public use.

I'm Speeding Because I Have To Poop!

Our private campsite had a dock to tie the boat to and a place to jump in and swim. From the dock, a path leading up a steep embankment ended on a flat piece of land, which made it easy for campers to set up sleeping and kitchen tents. The Canadian Shield rock bed was the perfect fire pit area.

Due to the steep incline from the water to the site, Rosie's Cabin was 100% private from passing boaters on the lake. This feature made it one of Dave's favourite places to camp.

That weekend, every noise made me jump. The wilderness is deadly quiet and even the slightest of noise from a little bug crawling over a leaf sounded like a moose traipsing through the bush.

Every time I would get startled, I'd say, "Dave, is that a bear?"

He was very patient with me and say, "No, Shawna, that's a mouse," or he'd point his flashlight at a small animal and say, "Shawna, it's a rabbit." or, "its just beaver swimming along the shore."

After the 53rd question regarding a noise in the bush, Dave firmly stated to me, "Shawna, I've been camping for 20 years in this area and never seen a friggin' bear, so enough with the bear questions!"

Oh boy! I had pushed him a little too far and didn't ask <u>that</u> question again.

Later that Saturday afternoon, we hooked up the portable solar shower to get cleaned up for a little frisky-time.

For those of you who have never showered naked in the wilderness, you really should try it. It's very liberating! Other than the odd mosquito that will bite you in places that no mosquito should ever venture, the experience is very un-inhibiting and free.

After our shower, we pulled the air mattresses out of the tent and set ourselves up on a nice flat rock in the sun. Since our site was so far up the hill from the lake, we knew we were safe from any gawking eyes.

After our romantic interlude, we took in some sun by laying on our backs soaking up the warm rays.

While I'm basking in the afterglow and taking in the warmth of the sun, Dave leaned over and quietly said to me, "Shawna, if you want to see a bear, get up *very slowly* and look to your right."

I did as Dave instructed and sure enough, approximately 50 feet away from us stood a fairly small black bear (we'll call him Blackie). Once I had seen enough, Dave quickly realized that Blackie wasn't going anywhere. In fact, he was starting to walk towards us.

This would ordinarily have been quite exciting; however, three things came to mind:

1. I was naked.
2. My clothes are nowhere near me.
3. We were at the furthest end of the site and nowhere near access to safe escape.

Mr. "Grizzly Adams", David, demonstrated his authority and control by getting up, with all his tackle swinging about and started to yell at Blackie. Unfortunately, he was not deterred.

I slowly rose off the air mattress and backed up towards the main area of camp, keeping an eye on Blackie the entire time. By this time, Dave had quickly backed up to get some pots from the kitchen area and had returned making all kinds of noises trying to get Blackie to retreat back into the woods. Yes, still naked.

Blackie went directly to our air mattresses to check them out and then sniffed out our tent. By this time we were backed right up to the kitchen area, which was close to the steep embankment where our boat was secured.

Unfortunately, our clothes were near our tent and the Blackie still occupied that space, therefore any chance to gain access to them was not an option.

Dave instructed me to go down to the boat, untie it, and wait for him there while he continued to scare Blackie away from camp. I agreed, but not before instructing him to take pictures of the bear before he joined me in the boat. I tossed him the camera and headed to the dock. Dave had a checkered button-up shirt, with cut-off sleeves hanging in a tree near the embankment, which I grabbed as I made my way down to the boat. I untied the boat and held onto the dock while I waited for Dave.

At this point, the shirt was held together with one hand while the other hand is grasping the dock to keep us from floating away.

I'm sure it was only a minute or less, but it seemed like 10 before I saw Dave make his way down to the dock, wearing only a pair of underwear. Apparently, Blackie had made its way to our kitchen area, backing Dave up as far as he could, leaving him no choice but to go down the embankment to the dock, almost naked.

Dave started the motor and we left the site, hoping that Blackie would eventually leave our site and retreat into the bush.

Once we left the dock, I had my hand free to do the buttons up on the shirt; however, this was Dave's camping shirt and it only had one button on it. Great! It didn't cover very much but was better than nothing!

A couple of people in their canoe paddled by us and asked us if everything was okay. We assumed that our lack of attire was the hint. We told the story of Blackie's visit and how we were waiting for him to retreat back into the bush.

When we got back to our site, we fully expected our food supply to be eaten and cooler emptied. It turns out that the bear must have just chowed down on a forest full of berries, as Blackie hadn't touched or eaten anything in our kitchen area. All of our food and beverages were fully accounted for.

We found it funny that Blackie spent most of his time by our air mattresses. Dave thought that since the bears were just out of hibernation, they were probably feeling a little frisky themselves.

Both Dave and I laughed at the irony of the experience: from my mom's comment; my excitement and constant pestering of Dave; Dave's resulting frustration with me; to the timing of the Blackie's arrival, we couldn't have planned this any better.

When we returned to Winnipeg, I couldn't wait to tell my folks the story. I left out "the frisky time" portion and told my folks a G-Rated version instead. However, I told my sister the real story and forgot to inform her that my folks only knew the G-rated version.

When discussing the incident with my folks, my sister re-iterated the real story and the discrepancy revealed itself. It's not that they would have minded. I was just trying to respect their generational thinking. Turns out it didn't matter to them. In fact, they thought it was pretty funny.

Of course, my mom freaked out about the bear, but I was home safe and sound and that's all that mattered to her. I think she might of said, "See, I told you so!"

It was an awesome experience to share with the love of my life.

Blackie

Baring It All

When Dave, his brother, Harvey, and I decided to go to Rincon de Guayabitos, Mexico for the very first time, we stayed at Decameron Los Cocos, an all-inclusive resort.

We landed in Puerto Vallarta on schedule and hopped on the shuttle bus for a 75-minute drive to the sleepy Mexican village. Harvey asked the bus driver if he could stop at a convenient store to grab some beverages for the road. It was hot and humid and we were thirsty. We had a couple of local Mexican beers on the bus, and arrived at our resort ready to take in the beach and sun.

After we grabbed a bite to eat and blew up our air mattresses, we hit the surf and sand.

Ordinarily, the Pacific Ocean is quite rough along the western shore, but due to the secluded bay the town is situated on, the beach line is protected making the water very calm. So calm, in fact, that I had a little nap on the air mattress in the water. I paddled my way out to the ropes, untied my bathing suit halter and retied it around my back to avoid tan lines. Faced down on the mattress, I held onto the ropes to keep me from floating away.

I assume at some point, I fell asleep and let go of the rope. Dave and Harvey had seen me drift in and wanted to be at the shore when I arrived.

All I remember is hitting something and getting startled. I didn't know what it was at the time, but the sudden stop was enough to flip me off the air mattress, which sent my bathing suit top south of the twins!

As I attempted to get my bearings back after having just woken up from a dead sleep, I realized that I had not tied my halter straps well enough and my twins were flopping all over the place.

Dave and Harvey just looked down and laughed at me.

One would think that Dave would be a little concerned that his brother witnessed my "girls gone wild," but he told me later that he wasn't that worried.

Neither of them offered to help me while I flailed about trying to readjust my bathing suit, which had somehow become twisted and unable to be put back on properly. They could have grabbed my air mattress to shield me from staring eyes, which were all over the place at this time since it was a national holiday and the beach was packed. Instead, they just let me figure it all out myself while I'm washed up on shore and flipping around like a fish out of water with sand in crevasses that took me all week to get rid of.

Keep in mind this is all happened in less than 30 seconds.

There are certain moments you don't want to share with your brother-in-law and this certainly qualified as one of those times. They on the other hand, thought this was very funny.

After I got myself dressed and re-oriented, the boys tried to talk me into going for a walk down the beach with them. I was so choked, I told them to go ahead and dove under an umbrella to seek shelter from the sun and gawking eyes. Again, I fell into a deep sleep.

When the boys returned from their walk, the sun had moved quite a bit, exposing me entirely to the UV rays which burnt me to a crisp. Again, I "ripped them a new one" and asked them why they didn't move the umbrella for me. They had explained that along their walk, they stopped for something to eat and had only returned moments before I awoke.

<u>Lessons learned</u>: Limit time in the sun on your first day; Wear SPF 70 sunscreen if you're not going to limit your time in the sun on your first day; never fall asleep on the ocean; secure your bathing suit at all times; cover up your body if you're going to fall asleep under an umbrella; and never rely on a man – regardless of who they are – to help you when the twins make an unexpected appearance.

56th Birthday
(Written by June)

Happy birthday dear Dave
Happy birthday to you
56 is still young
Plus you're real active too

The timing is perfect
Around a fire you'll be
Celebrating your birthday
With the boys and a whiskey

The next day you'll hunt
But I'll warn you right now
That my memo went out
To all the bulls and the cows

It'll be a great birthday
Reminiscing with the guys
In the most beautiful setting
And under the starlit skies!

Conch-A Smell It?

"As mentioned in a previous story, my mom, dad, sister, niece, cousin, husband, and I traveled to Varadero, Cuba, for a weeklong vacation to an all-inclusive resort.

While taking a walk along the beach one morning, Dave and I encountered a fisherman who was trying to sell us some of his local catch. Since we were staying in an all-inclusive resort, we had no method of cooking the fish and politely declined.

He then asked us if we were interested in purchasing a fresh Conch shell that he recently caught, for approximately $10 Canadian. Conch is a common name that is applied to a number of different mediums to large-sized sea snails or their shells. The term generally applies to large sea snails with shells that come to a point at both ends. Conch shells are seen for sale all the time in Mexico. Nice, fresh, shiny shells that you put up to your ear to hear "the ocean". Ah, now you know what kind of shell I'm talking about, right?

We brought the shell into our room and washed it out, as it was slimy on the inside. Both Dave and I did not realize the difference between a fresh conch and one that is ready for sale at the local market. We believed the snail might have been alive shortly before we bought it and was slowly dying in our care. After a day in our hotel room, we picked up an odor that Dave discovered was coming from the shell, so he put it outside on our balcony to dry it out and give it some fresh air. We kept it on the balcony until our departure day.

At one point, I picked it up and started to cluck. I said, "Yuk, that smells like a rotten crotch"!

The day we were heading home, Dave asked me if I really wanted to take this home as it stunk, albeit, not as smelly as it had been earlier in the week. I had a perfect place at the lake in mind and really wanted to get it there. Reluctantly, Dave packed it in our carry-on baggage, wrapping it up in many layers of newspapers and several plastic bags. I felt quite confident that this would contain whatever odor was left.

At the airport, our family met up by the departure gate.

I'm Speeding Because I Have To Poop!

My niece Robyn starts sniffing the air and says, "Phoi, gross! I think I stink like a rotten v-gigi."

Dave glared at me and we started to giggle. The giggle turned into a burst of laughter, which nobody understood. Once we gained some composure, I explained that it wasn't HER that smelled like a rotting corpse, but rather the item we packed in our carry-on.

At that point Dave said, "That's it Shawna, we can't bring this on the plane. It's going to stink up the cabin."

Since I *really* wanted to bring this home, I suggested that we put the carry-on in an upper compartment (instead of at our feet like we usually do), far away from our seats. I explained that people usually don't go into the upper compartments during the flight so it would be contained. Dave reluctantly agreed.

When it was time to board, Dave gave me one last opportunity to dump the shell, but I insisted that the carry-on luggage already smelled bad and we had to bring it home regardless since there were other items in the bag too.

As we walked down the ramp to board the plane, we could both smell the carry-on luggage and it was bad! We boarded the plane and, as suggested, Dave put the bag in the far end of the plane's upper compartment area.

When it was time to retrieve our bag in Winnipeg, Dave opened up the over-head bin and was overcome with the foul odor from the conch shell.

We laughed all the way out of the plane and never looked back to see people's reaction.

When we got home, we put the shell in our unheated back porch to dry and freshen it up. In May, we brought it to the lake and it remains down at the lake gazebo, exactly where I wanted it.

<u>Side note</u>: When writing this story, I was concerned about the legalities of importing the conch shell into Canada. I did some research and discovered that it is perfectly legal to bring them into Canada. They do, however, recommend that they be washed out with bleach prior to travelling. This is something I wish we would have known in Cuba!

Mexican Road Trip

As you know by now, Dave and I prefer the independent bungalow-style holidays as opposed to all-inclusive vacationing; however, Dave had been working harder than usual this particular year and it was time for him to be pampered. This was the same year that our family went to Cuba together in late January, making this our second all-inclusive vacation in the winter of 2011. After searching on-line for something different, we found a small, secluded resort, an approximately 60-minute drive from Manzanillo, on the west coast of Mexico.

The resort turned out to be a complete disappointment and we wished we would not of gone. While our room was the best part of the holiday, the beach was short and the ocean full of jellyfish, which washed up on the shore nightly. The meal selections were terrible and the bartenders were greedy, although they made a killer margarita. The swim-up bar was incredible, but the resort was empty, leaving only a few people to socialize with. The secluded resort made it impossible to tour the Manzanillo area without calling upon their extremely expensive local taxi service. We felt captive and had cabin fever almost immediately.

My sister Nancy and her partner, Jim, planned to be in the Puerto Vallarta (PV) area a couple days after our arrival in Mexico and stayed in a condo by the main PV marina. My folks arrived a couple days later and also stayed in their condo. Before any of us headed to Mexico, Nancy and Jim asked us if we were interested in staying with them for a day or two, however we couldn't commit right away. We wanted to experience our resort first, and if we liked it, we planned on staying there for the duration of our holiday.

After spending a couple days at our resort, we jumped at their offer and planned to head north and spend a day or two with them and our folks.

Our challenge was getting to Puerto Vallarta from Manzanillo, but after some negotiations, we agreed upon $17,500 pesos including tip ($160 Canadian) for a one-way trip with a local taxi.

I'm Speeding Because I Have To Poop!

The taxi picked us up on time and we were on our way to another adventure in majestic Mexico. The ride was beautiful along the western coast with a great view of the Pacific Ocean much of the time.

We arrived in Puerto Vallarta before noon and in complete awe of the accommodations Nancy, Jim, and my folks had. The 3-bedroom, 3-bathroom, wrap-around balcony overlooking a massive eternity pool, and the view of Banderas Bay took our breath away. I wanted to stay here for the next week!

We spent the day getting served by pool staff, floating around and walking on the beach, checking out the ships in the marina. It was a perfect day. About dinnertime, my sister informed me that a friend and husband were also going to be spending a night or two with them and that she was short on beds. She suggested that we sleep on couches in the living room, but Dave and I had a different idea.

When Nancy and Jim's friends arrived, all 8 of us went to a fabulous restaurant in the marina, for a phenomenal dinner, starting with a free tequila shot, and ending with a "brown cow" banana split. I think the tequila and sun challenged Jim's dexterity and balance as Dave and Dad had to walk him back to the condo before dinner was over.

When it was time for bed, Nancy started to get the couches ready but Dave and I suggested the idea we had thought of earlier in the day. We put two, luxurious loungers on the balcony together, covered them with sheets and bedding, and slept outside overlooking the Pacific Ocean while we listened to the waves sweep onto the shore. It was the perfect accommodation and we didn't want to be anywhere else but there.

The next morning, we all ventured down to a fantastic waffle house in the marina for breakfast.

Dave and I bid the family farewell and hopped up a bus to the main bus depot. We purchased a one-way ticket on a luxury bus line, which dropped us off on the highway, 3 kilometers from our resort. It was a challenge getting the driver to understand where we wanted to be dropped off, but with a few charades and a handy translation book, we figured it out.

It was an expensive 24-hour diversion from our Manzanillo holiday, but well worth it. We got to spend time with Nancy, Jim, and my folks and made a little adventure out of it along the way. This is what life's all about. Got to keep it interesting!!

From left to right: Jim, Nancy, Dave, Shawna, Mom, and Dad enjoying pool time at Jim and Nancy's condo in Puerto Vallarta

Mexican Torture Chamber

Almost every year, we return to Rincon de Guayabitos for a winter holiday.

One of the benefits of returning to the same place every year is that you get to know the local shops and vendors. I have come to know Yolanda, who owns a massage and manicure shop along the main street in Guayabitos. Yolanda and I have chatted about her coming to visit us in Canada and we've opened up our home when she's ready for her Canadian experience.

Back at home, I have connections to get nail lacquer at a substantial discount compared to what Yolanda has to pay in Mexico. She asked me if I could pick up a variety of nail lacquers in exchange for a manicure, pedicure, and a full body massage for both David and me.

Thanks to the fine ladies at the distributor, I collected over 30 bottles of new and opened bottles of nail lacquers and strengtheners for a fraction of the regular price.

Upon our arrival in Guayabitos, I dropped off the large selection of products and booked Dave and I massages. I arranged to have my manicure and pedicure done shortly before returning home to Winnipeg.

Dave and I arrived for our massages and were escorted through a door, which immediately lead into a narrow hallway. The hallway was short with two massage table bays to the right. At the end of the hall, there was washroom. Other than the exterior door, there were no other doors in this area; only floor length curtains separated each room, including the washroom.

I was asked to lay down on the first massage table, closest to the exit, as Dave stretched out, face down, on the table closest to the washroom. The ladies asked both of us to take off *all* of our clothes. I'm used to this as I always take my clothes off for massages at home, but Dave, only having had one massage in his life, wasn't overly comfortable with disrobing completely. He did as he was instructed though.

At first, my massage therapist started on my neck and back area and moved her way down to my legs quite quickly. Her touch was so soft, I was wondering if she was actually a massage therapist or if she was a stand-in for a sick employee. I wasn't impressed.

Apparently, she was only warming up. Once she returned up to my upper body, she started applying more pressure and could feel the areas that she felt needed some work. All of the sudden, I could feel this elbow grinding into my back and I swear one of my lungs collapsed and a rib popped out. The pain took my breath away as I tensed up.

She let out a little giggle and asked, "Too much?"

"Si," I replied.

When she got to my butt, all gloves were off and she was digging into muscle that my body forgot I had. Have you ever been walking backwards and hit the corner of desk or table with one of your butt cheeks? Imagine that moment – TIMES TEN! That is exactly how she was attacking my butt cheeks. Pressing, twisting, and grinding like my arse was the face of her ex-boyfriend that she just caught cheating with her best friend. I don't know what my arse ever did to her, but she was in full-out revenge mode.

After beating the crap out of my butt, she put the python grip on my calves. When she wrapped both hands around my calves and started pulling towards my ankles, I thought my reflexes were going to kick her in the face. Maybe that's just what I wanted to do! She squeezed and pulled at the same time as she dug her thumbs into the calf muscle and I almost screamed. She pulled down so hard, I swear I grew two extra inches in that hour.

What the heck? Why am I being punished? This is a torture chamber, not a massage spa!

By the time she got to my feet, I was exhausted and tense in anticipation of what this Mexican mafia master was going to do to me next. This anxiety was not without cause and as she started on my feet, it darn near sent me into orbit. Her thumbs connected with pressure points that I was convinced would cripple me for the rest of my holiday if not the remainder of my life.

While I lay there, as my tears dropped one by one on the floor, I started writing this part of the book in my head. God willing, I'd survive the Mexican Torture Chamber and be able to put this experience in writing.

When she was finished crushing my feet, she asked me to flip over onto my back where she proceeded to cut off the blood flow of my arms. She used the same crippling procedure as she had done on my calves. She grabbed with two hands, pressed down hard and pulled towards my toes.

Fungola (as my girlfriend Susan would say)! Holey moley! Kill me now! I did it! I'll confess! Just stop the torture!!! Honestly, if I thought I could move any part of my body quickly, I would have kicked her in the gut and broke her hands to prevent her from inflicting this kind of torture on another human being. I would have declared self-defense. After all, she was killing me! I say this being the most non-violent person you'd meet!

Just as I'm plotting my ninja move, I heard a loud noise. Since it was quiet in the massage area, any noise seemed loud. It was enough to distract my pity party and revenge plot I was silently hatching. It sounded like someone was filling up a big pail of water with lots of velocity and pressure coming from the tap. That went on for about 15 seconds, followed by a really loud fart! At that moment, I realized that it was someone peeing in the bathroom, ending it all with a ginormous anal explosion.

That was it for me! I had been pent up in the torture chamber for an hour, every single muscle ached and I was probably tenser than when I had walked in. I definitely wanted to cry some more, but when the fart let loose in the bathroom, all I could do was laugh and I could not stop. My laugh turned into hysteria and my tears were now emotions from the entire experience.

My massage therapist started off with a giggle and ended up laughing with me. She eventually put a cloth over my face so that she could focus on finishing my massage. To me, the massage was finished because by then, *I was done!*

From my massage area, I could also hear Dave laughing too. Later he told me that he was laughing at my hysteria more than the spontaneous combustion in the washroom next to his massage table.

I guess I'm a sucker for punishment because after the massage, I gave her a tip for almost killing me. I waited for Dave to crawl out of his chamber. While waiting, I noticed the list of massages that were available: relaxation, therapeutic, and deep tissue massage. I honestly didn't pay that much attention when these massages were booked but clearly we received the deep tissue massage and were not consulted upon arrival. We would have chosen the relaxation, but the deed was done and I had survived!

When Dave limped out of the back room, he told me that at one point during his massage, he thought his therapist was standing on her elbows digging into his back. As if that weren't enough, he was convinced that she had her 300 lb. Mexican mafia boyfriend doing the same. With his head stuffed into the small face hole on the massage table, he was paralyzed from his eyebrows to his toenails.

Dave summed it up by saying, "I would rather have been mugged on the beach by a gang of banditos. It would have been less painful."

We will stick to having our massages at home, where the therapists don't combine massage and hit-man classes to become certified.

Thankfully, my manicure and pedicure were much more enjoyable; however, I truly believe that Yolanda got the better end of the deal this time.

Chapter III

Just Me

THE SECOND MIDDLE CHILD

These stories and poems have either been written to me or are my personal experiences.

Shawna J Peterson

40th Birthday
(Written by June)

40 years ago
You were born at St. B
Making it three girls
In our fam-i-l-y

Beautiful blue eyes
And a smile to match
The blondest of hair
One day a great catch

Dave is the lucky one'
With who whom you share your life
When in Las Vegas
He made you his wife

Together you spend
Much time at the lake
Laughing with friends
And floating till you bake

Let's not forget Eric
Who turned out so great
Your love and devotion
Has really paid off (sorry I couldn't think of a good word that rhymed with great)

I'm Speeding Because I Have To Poop!

On a less serious note
One thing I must say
YOUR BIG BOOBS WILL SHRINK
AND HANG DOWN ONE DAY

Happy birthday dear Shawna
Happy birthday dear sis
I'm so happy to be partying
On your 40th and get ripped

Bottoms up!

I used to work for a company that made commissary-type items such as sandwiches, pizza pops, pizzas, perogies, and cabbage rolls for small mom-and-pop grocery stores, as well as large grocery store chains.

To fully appreciate this story, you need to know the layout of the office and commissary areas.

As soon as you came in the front doors, you would see a large open area where both the supervisor and I sat. Off that open area were 2 offices, a boardroom, a single bathroom for office staff, and the door going into the commissary area. My supervisor's desk was directly beside the single washroom and my desk was beside the commissary entrance. The commissary area had their own washroom, tucked into a corner just off their change room.

One day, my stomach was not happy and the grumblings overtook my concentration. I knew *I had to go* and it wasn't going to be pretty. The thought of using the office washroom wasn't an option as I knew from all the commotion in my tummy that it was going to be quite noisy and absolutely going to smell like something had died, decayed, and rotted. The commissary washroom was my only choice. Not only did it offer me a more private place to conduct my potty business, but it also was an opportunity to take an enormous anonymous crap where nobody would know who did "the deed". Thankfully, the afternoon break was over and everyone was back to work so I wouldn't be rushed or interrupted, leaving plenty of time for the odor to get sucked up by the exhaust fan before the next person had to use it.

I went into the washroom, sat down, and started to make my deposit when I heard someone in the change room area, walking towards the washroom. Instinctively, I leaned forward to ensure the door was locked and the unimaginable happened.

The door opened, I looked up with my arse straight in the air, pants down around the ankles, stretching my arm to push in the lock button, and there stood one of the owners, staring right at me. He quickly slammed the door. I decided right then and there that I was going to live in that washroom for the rest of my life. There are no words to describe how embarrassed I was. I had no idea how I was going to return to my desk and work for the rest of the day. So, I sat in there for quite a while pondering my future as a toilet fixture, as I couldn't comprehend leaving that room, *ever*. Eventually, I had to return to my desk.

Looking back, I should have just used the office washroom and faced whatever humiliation comes with taking a big crap at work. At least no body parts would have been hanging out!

I couldn't look that particular owner in the eyes for weeks after that incident. Truly, I'm not sure which one of us was more embarrassed. We never did talk about it. Even after I left the company and saw him periodically in other environments, this subject was taboo.

That was my most embarrassing work moment ever…well, maybe not….read on!!

Do You Hear What I Hear?

No, this is not about a Christmas carol!

One day my employer asked me to sit in a provincial government meeting room during an emergency event. The large room occupied employees from other federal and provincial departments as well as emergency organizations.

The meeting room was not air-conditioned and it was very warm with large fans blowing re-circulated air within the room. I sat in the last row and had several very loud fans directly behind me.

The environment of the room was quiet as people were reporting on the status of the event to their respective departments and organizations. Because the fans were quite noisy, one needed to talk fairly loud for the person next to you to hear.

In this noisy environment, surely nobody would hear me fart, right? So, I let one rip and it felt so amazing! I had been holding them all day and I just had to ease the pressure, so I let a few more go. I knew that they would probably be noisy if the fans weren't on, but I was safe since there were plenty of fans going in the room at once. I should have picked up on some of the stares I was getting. Instead, I would just smile back and continue to work (and farted if I had to).

When representing your department, you are expected to communicate with the Director who sits up at the front of the room. At the end of the day, I received a request from my office, which required me to speak with the Director, so I walked up to the front of the room and approached him.

Once I reached the front, I turned completely red and stopped dead in my tracks. It was perfectly quiet from the front of the room. You couldn't hear the fans, but you could hear people talking and typing on their computer. I realized at that very moment that my gas was likely heard by everyone in the room, and most certainly by folks sitting up at the front. This would definitely explain the interesting looks I got that afternoon.

While I'm sure my "oh crap" facial expression did not go unnoticed, I obtained the answer from the Director and high-tailed it back to my office.

I usually take embarrassing moments like these with a grain of salt, however even though nobody said anything directly to me, I'm certain I did not make our office look very good that day. THAT, I regret.

Lessons learned: Never take a noisy room for granted AND I need to invest in a de-gassing product!!

I did warn you, at the beginning of this book, that this was bathroom material, right?

40 "Something" Birthday
(Written by June)

Roses are red
Violets are blue
Your birthday is here
Now what will you do?

Let's celebrate in Pen
With Nancy & Jim
Maybe go to the casino
And go out on a limb

Of course we'll have wine
And lots of good food
But we will watch our diets
Cause that's what we do

Happy birthday dear Shawna
Happy birthday to you
Enjoy your day
That is what you need to do

Guilty with an Explanation

After work, I headed to the dog groomers to pick up our 2 dogs, Bailey and Mr. McGoo.

When I got to the vet, the dogs weren't quite ready and I had to go to the bathroom. I thought to myself, "Mmmm, I think I can wait, but I probably should go while I'm here. Nahhh, I can wait." So I did.

After the dogs have been at the groomers all day, I would normally take them for a little walk so they can poop and pee before putting them in the car. That day was different, as our plans were to head to the lake as soon as I got home and I didn't want any delays. We only lived seven minutes from the groomers and I figured both the dogs and I could make it home before reaching the danger zone.

I had almost passed the grocery store when I remembered I needed oyster sauce for marinated veggies that we wanted to make for our guests at the lake. I swung into the left parking lane and ran into the store, really needing to go.

I ran up and down the aisles, trying to find the oyster sauce, which turned out to be the first aisle I had looked at. I was doing the side-to-side shuffle at the cashier stand and was starting to sweat. I should have just gone to the bathroom there but I was in a *rush* and just kept clenching. By this point, you know it wasn't #1, right?

I *ran* to the truck, jumped in, started it up and pulled away. After a few seconds, a foul odor hit me square in the nostril and as I looked in the back seat of the truck, Bailey and Mr. McGoo were quietly staring at me, sitting beside two very large and mushy piles of crap.

Three things immediately came to my mind:

1. I should have listened to my gut and took my own poop in the store since my dogs felt it necessary to do the same.
2. I should have immediately returned to the store and used the washroom.
3. The smell of crap made me have to go EVEN MORE.

I was starting to "prairie dog" and wasn't sure if I was going to be able to hold it. I clenched as hard as I could and, so far, I was winning the race!

I was so happy that I got *all* green lights within a few blocks of the house, but I got stuck behind a really slow driver about 200 meters from home, so I floored it to pass her. For about three seconds, I was pedal to the metal then signaled back in when I was approaching the street to our house.

Just as I was about to turn left onto my street, this guy runs out in the middle of the road waving his hands. I'm so close to home and ready to unleash the crap of all craps in my pants and I have to talk to this guy? Really? Doesn't he know that I *have* to get home, RIGHT NOW?

That's it! "I'm going to crap my pants right here," I thought, as I simply could not hold on much longer.

Turns out I got caught in a speed trap and I almost ran over a police office!!! They clocked me doing 67 in a 50 (for the three seconds while I passed that ole bitty who couldn't drive more than 20 kilometers an hour) while I was trying to prevent a big dung from falling out my drawers. Jeepers creepers!!! Really? I had broken a sweat that rivaled the bubonic plague and if I didn't take this crap soon, I was going to pass out.

The officer asked me if there was a particular reason I was speeding to which I replied very firmly, "My dogs took a crap in the back seat of my truck and I'm about to take one in the front if I don't get to a bathroom in the next 45 seconds."

I pointed to my house and told him that I lived 2 seconds away. He informed me that I could not go home and instructed me to pull over to the other side of the road. He suggested that I park and ask to use the washroom in the hair salon, located on the same street.

"Follow me home and give me my ticket or let me go home to take a dump and I promise I will come right back, but I have to go <u>RIGHT NOW</u>," I begged.

He wouldn't budge. So I did as instructed while clenching my butt, which I'm certain had started to dilate. Nothing was backing up and the force was overly intense. I had to wait for him to get to my truck to give him my registration and driver's license, so I figured that was a good a time as any to pick up the pile of crap from the back seat of the truck.

He approached me while I was putting the dog's deposits it into a plastic baggie. I felt like turning around, dropping my drawers, and dumping right into the plastic baggie just to make him feel like a complete idiot – but I didn't. Instead I told him that this was no picnic for me and how pissed off I was that he wouldn't let me go home to crap in peace and with some dignity. I threw him my driver's license and registration, slammed the door, and ran into the hairdressers with a baggie full of poop, asking them if I could use their bathroom. Before I got a response, I was in the bathroom, slammed the door, and had the loudest, earth-moving dump of my life (if I were telling you this story, I would use sound affects). Once I released the goods, I sat in the bathroom on the crapper and laughed and laughed and laughed.

My mind was going a million miles an hour thinking:

1. YEAH! I didn't crap my pants!
2. That cop must be peeing himself laughing.
3. I have to walk out of here with everyone in salon knowing and hearing that I almost crapped myself.
4. Fungola. I got a friggin' speeding ticket!!
5. We're getting to the lake late – ah nuts!
6. YEAH... I didn't crap my pants (again)!

I walked out of the bathroom and thanked them for the use of it. I also apologized if I caused a disruption and went back to my truck.

The police officer took forever to get back to the truck and once he did, I said, "You know, I have a 16 year old stepson and pride myself on setting a good example for him. I normally don't speed, but *clearly* I was in a time of need and was trying to get home, but hey, shit happens!" The officer laughed out loud and told me that he *had* to give me a ticket because of how fast he'd clocked me, but recommended that I should contest the ticket.

Years ago, I had a bumper sticker made for my car that says, "I'm Speeding Because I Have To Poop" (thus, the name of this book), and I haven't got a ticket since!! Not sure if the two are related.

P.S. I plead "guilty with an explanation". The magistrate had a very difficult time keeping a straight face as she was reading the notes the police officer took. She let me off with a $100 court cost fine and no demerits on my license. See, it pays to be honest while humiliating yourself six ways to Sunday!

The actual bumper sticker that is on Shawna's back window of her car

I'm Speeding Because I Have To Poop!

SHAWNA'S (49th birthday)
(Written by June)

Happy Birthday dear Shawna
Happy birthday dear sis
Next year you'll be 50
And we'll all be in Las Vegas

The guys will be hunting
While we're playing the slots
And in between shows
We'll be doing a few shots

But for now something else
Is coming up for you
It's the Grey Cup of course
And Teresa's excited too

So for now you must concentrate
And take care of yourself
You must blast out that kidney stone
And get back to good health

So have a good birthday
It's your special time
Kick back and relax
With a nice glass of wine

Chapter IV

My Bestie, Teresa

Teresa and Shawna

It Depends!

(An actual text message exchange between Shawna and Teresa – only true friends could have this exchange).
Dates have been omitted purposely.

11:30 AM

Teresa: I was planning to treat you to a Bomber game for your birthday. What should I ask for when I go get the tickets?

Shawna: Awe. That's so nice of you. Thank you!!!! Ask for the $60 Buddy vouchers for two tickets. We play against Calgary so we are likely to get our arses handed to us. Hey, should we do the <u>diaper</u> test this game? I need to include that story in my book!!!

Teresa: Lmao! I'll have to get back to you on that one. "Depends" on the weather lol!! Touch base later...have a good day. Ciao ☺!!!!

5:45 PM (SAME DAY)

Shawna: If you want me to cheer for team, you will need to wear a diaper and pee your pants with me – hey I'm not above bribery!! Lmao

Teresa: If they play like this and we're together I may very well need those diapers. lol!!

10:30 AM (NEXT DAY)

Shawna: I can wear a diaper on Sat and catch my stones as they fall out at the game. The thought of bringing a strainer to the stadium didn't sit so well with me. Now I can just "go go go" and they'll be safe and sound tucked away. Of course it might feel like I'm sitting on a gravel pit till I get home!! Have you stopped laughing yet??

Teresa: Oh my. Just read this. Are you serious? A strainer? Diaper it is then...lol!! Are you sure you still want to go?

I'm Speeding Because I Have To Poop!

Shawna: Yes of course. I am going to have to drink copious amounts of liquid to keep my kidneys pumping and get the stones out.

8:45AM (ANOTHER DAY LATER)

Shawna: You're not going to believe what a colleague said to me? "Shawna... I'm worried about this plan of yours... What happens if you leak through at the football game? I think you should test it out first! How about sitting in the bosses chair and try going? If it doesn't leak out, you're good to go"!!
Can you imagine being the boss and reading that in my book? I almost died laughing BUT I'm going to do it!!! Boss will never know till it's all over!!! Great pre-amble to the story!!!

Teresa: Let me know how your test goes. I would put a drop cloth down just in case. lol

NOON (NEXT DAY)

Shawna: Ok. I've been wearing this damn diaper all day and I can't pee in it. Even when I really really have to go... I sit in my boss's chair and relax and focus on just peeing and it gets so far, then.... Nothing! I'm not sure it's possible to pee on purpose unless you medically can't hold it. Interesting experiment before Saturday! The weird thing is that I really have to go. I think I'm getting pee-pot, as I haven't gone all day!! Pee pot is when you don't pee and your tummy bloats!

Teresa: Oh my...Lmao! I'm at our Tradeshow and just burst out laughing!!

1:15PM (SAME DAY)

Shawna: Well you will laugh harder now!! I decided to check out the diaper and see if perhaps I HAD peed and just not felt it. Nope! Nothing!

	I thought I'd try something different. I sat on the toilet with my diaper ON and voila! She let loose! What a weird feeling. Not sure what to do now!
Holey crap these things are heavy when they're wet! I can see how babies and seniors alike don't want to keep them on once you've emptied your bladder in them.
I don't think I smell but I probably shouldn't keep these on. Mmmm. I need to check and see if I leaked through so I'm going to feel around now. Standby for results!!
Teresa:	You're killing me!! Lmao!!!

A MINUTE OR SO LATER

Shawna: Dry as a bone!!! It'll work for Saturday providing I can give it a little space to come out. It'll keep our keesters nice and warm too. Wear baggy pants!!

ANOTHER COUPLE MINUTES LATER

Shawna: Disposal: this is probably the most awkward part - I wrapped the diaper in toilet paper and honest to goodness, it looks like I'm throwing out an infant wrapped up in a swaddling bundle! It takes up the entire feminine disposal bucket!! The end!!

Teresa: Ttyl! Still Lmao!!

END OF TEXT MESSAGE CONVERSATION

Side note: The diaper test idea was originally born several years ago at a cold November play-off Bomber Game.

November games required us to wear snowmobile suits or ski pants, which caused everyone seating on the benches to be squished together. It was a challenge getting to the washrooms as everyone in the row had to stand up, hold their blankets and hot chocolate while we waddled through to the stairs. As well, taking off layers of clothing in a small bathroom stall was not fun. If we wore a diaper, we would eliminate those issues.

<u>Lesson learned:</u> It is not possible to pee your pants on purpose. Your mind will not let your body do it. We, therefore, did not wear a diaper to the game, but the test was really funny. The colleague who suggested the test was sworn to secrecy until this book was released.

Caterpillar's Revenge

Every year, my girlfriend Teresa and I have a girl's weekend at our trailer in Pinawa. This trip was one of the first ones.

When we arrived on Saturday morning, we noticed that there were a *lot* of those green/black furry caterpillars. Initially, the caterpillars were just a nuisance, falling from trees, but it didn't take us long to realize that it was more of an infestation than just an abnormally high caterpillar year.

We thought a bike ride away from the site would be a nice change, as these furry creatures were everywhere by the trailer. The bikes were located underneath the tongue of the 5th wheel trailer, which was enclosed and doubled as a storage shed. When I went under the tongue to get the bikes, caterpillars were falling on my head. I screamed and squirmed to do this as quickly as possible while getting completely freaked out with the sheer number of these furry things crawling down the back of my shirt. The caterpillars had already started making cocoons under the bike seats and in the ceiling of the storage area. Blah!!! Gives me the creeps just thinking about it again.

We discovered quickly that it was going to be a quiet bike ride as the caterpillars hung from trees and went into your mouth if you spoke. We wore sunglasses so that our furry fren-emies would not end up in our eyes. It was completely disgusting. This was not fun, so we retreated back to the trailer.

Fungola! The screen room was completely covered with the pesky worms! Since we had to get past them to access the inside of the screen room and trailer, we quickly opened the door and rushed in. Not before many of them landed on our head and down the back of our shirt again. Geee-rosss!

After we took care of each other and swept then killed each and every caterpillar that landed on us, we went on the offensive attack and vowed to wipe out this army if it was the last thing we did. They had messed with a girl's weekend and were going to regret it! We made a mixture to spray down the screen room and killed the peckers.

I'm Speeding Because I Have To Poop!

We found out that this was not as easy a task as we had hoped. The mixture consisted of sunlight soap and water. Once you spray the mixture on them, they can't breathe through the coat of soapy water and they die. We would spray the screens every 10 minutes and a new regiment of the army would march up and replace the ones we killed.

You could hear them fall on the top of the awning and in places you could actually see part of the ground move as the kajillion of them attacked with vengeance. It was horrible.

As soon as the sun started to go behind the trees, they retreated and found warmth on the bark of trees, exposed to the sun, and stayed there until the next day. Some of them decided to honker down in the site and continue to torture us into the evening. We flicked those little peckers onto the wood burning stove and watched them sizzle and get crispy. You know, I normally love all animals and bugs but this was just plain creepy. They had to be destroyed at any cost.

We had a nice fire with our friends until midnight.

It was bedtime. As usual, I gave up my bedroom for my girlfriend's comfort. I love sleeping in the screen room and intended on sleeping there until the infestation of the caterpillars overtook it. There was no way I was going to sleep one wink in there, so I opted to sleep on the hide-a-bed in the trailer.

The hide-a-bed was not very comfortable so we used a foam-bedding topper to give it extra support. The foam bed topper was stored underneath the bench seat of the table set in the screen room. Yep… we had to go back in there to get it.

Teresa and I were both very creeped out and I was extremely tense as I lifted the cushion off and to my relief, there were no caterpillars under the cushion. Now, I had to lift the plywood seat off in order to get into the storage area. I was so nervous and as stiff as the plywood I had to lift off.

Teresa stayed in the trailer and peaked her head outside the door and watched me. She giggled a bit and teased me with noises as I put my hands on the plywood edges and started to lift the seat. I open the plywood hinge and all I saw was the foam bed topper all rolled up nicely. I let out a deep and heavy sigh of relief as I had imagined it being full of tent caterpillars and cocoons. I felt like a fool that I was so worried about what I would find in there. After all, it's a sealed seating booth with four sides of plywood and nowhere for the critters to get in. I very confidently lifted up the rolled up bed topper and a million fuzzy creatures fell to the floor.

I let out one *blood curdling* scream, jumped up on one of the chairs, and started to babble in what sounded like 47 different languages.

My neighbours at the lake (Ted and his brother, Larry) shouted out to me but I was unable to speak. Thinking there was a bear in our site and not knowing exactly what was going on, they ran over carrying a hot poker stick from the fire and a club-style flashlight. They both ran so fast, they tripped over the big pile of sand that was in the middle of the driveway. While attempting to talk me down from the lawn chair in the middle of the screen room, I babbled and cried while I explained my dilemma.

In the meantime, Lorna and Llowyin (Ted and Larry's wives) yelled over and asked if everything was okay. I was in hysterics and the brothers still didn't know what was wrong.

Finally, I was able to explain the caterpillars in the bed foamy and they understood why I was upset, but didn't seem as freaked out. I shook so bad that Larry took me by the shoulders and forced me to focus on what had actually fallen out of the bed foam topper. They were poplar seeds that had been stored in there by squirrels or chipmunks. Honestly, I still don't know how they got in there. In my defense, poplar seeds also are long fuzzy things and in the dark they looked like caterpillars.

I *instantly* went calm and then said, "Well don't I feel like biggest loser in the campground," and then proceeded to laugh and cry, then laugh.

Ted and Larry got a chuckle out of it and returned to their site to explain what happened to their wives.

Teresa and I laughed together, uncontrollably, for about 30 minutes. We went to bed laughing and I swear we were still laughing as we drifted off to sleep.

The next day, we went for a walk and people asked if we heard that scream late at night. The folks we talked to thought there was a bunch of bears in the campground. I just pretended that I didn't hear a thing and kept this story to myself, except occasionally when we would tell it around a campfire with our friends.

Oooh... That Feels So Good

One cold autumn day, Teresa and I visited the cemetery that her dad was interned.

After we said a little prayer and walked around the property, we headed to the hospital to spend a bit of time with her mom, who was also ailing.

Before we went to her mom's room, Teresa needed to use the washroom so I wasted a bit of time in the gift shop. We agreed to meet at the main elevator and go up to see her mom together. After a few minutes, Teresa wasn't at the elevator and I was still chilly from the cold. I assumed I had time to quickly warm them up by running them under warm water in the washroom.

I went into the washroom and started running the warm water. When it became warm, I gently ran my hands under the tap and started saying things out loud, like, "Ooooohhh, that feels so good. That feels so good, soooooo good! I'm warming up now. Oh ya, that's better."

I asked her, "Teresa, are you almost done in there?" No response. Huh? I looked towards the stall and noticed a red jacket through the small crack of the door.

Immediately I thought, "Mmmm. I don't think Teresa was wearing red," and that's when I saw it – the urinal.

I realized I was in the men's washroom making all kinds of interesting noises while my hands were warming up. I made a beeline out of there and saw Teresa by the elevator waiting for me. She asked where I was and I almost peed myself telling her the story.

When we arrived at her mom's room, Teresa's sister was there. We told both of them the story which provided a nice light moment in this dark time for Teresa's family.

I sometimes wonder what the poor soul in that bathroom stall was thinking while I was in there. I think he likely told that story from a different perspective to whomever he was visiting in the hospital that day.

49th Birthday

(Written by Shawna)

Happy Birthday Teresa
Happy Birthday "T"
I'm so glad that you're 49 now
Cuz you're so much older than me!!

I know this year will be so great
But just wait until our big "FIVE-0"
When we celebrate "Vegas" style
Ka-Ching Ka-Ching – then we go broke

Olé - Un, Deux, Trois

Teresa, and I were at the trailer in Pinawa for another girls weekend. We were having a CFL marathon, watching every game from Friday to Saturday night. We kept seeing a commercial, advertising French beer. The setting of the commercial was a rooftop social gathering with snippets of people in small groups talking in French. The camera would pan across the rooftop catching a few words of each conversation. None of these sentences made any sense, as they were random French words put together. I never really understood the meaning of the commercial.

All of the sudden, I had to fart; so I did and followed up with my usual declaration, complete with hand motions and said, "Olé!"

Teresa started a chain of events that has now become a farting production. Whenever one of us farts, we now say, "Olé" (complete with circular pointing hand motions), followed up by alternating random French words, like:

le croissant	un deux trois
la moustache	pardon moi
voulez-vous coucher avec moi ce soir	qu'est-ce que c'est
escargot	au revoir
mon amie	se il vous plait
Pepé Le Pew (if it's a stinker)	je ne sais quoi
bonjour	merci
bon appétit	à la carte
cochon (complete with snorting noises)	bonsoir

It doesn't matter where we are or what conversation we're engaged in; If one of us

lets'er rip, we pause, go through all of the motions and words, then resume our conversation. It's hilarious and sometimes we pause to laugh and other times we simply carry on with whatever we were doing. Teresa has upped her game and tries to get in as many words as she can, before I can even say one. We don't use all the words all the time, but try to get as many in as we can think of within five seconds. Even if other people are around, we go on autopilot.

I love my friends and all their quirkiness. Their influences, coupled by a bizarre television commercial, have created a farting tradition that will be in place for years and years to come!

I'm pretty sure at the beginning of the book I warned the reading audience that this is bathroom material, right?

Time To "Play Ball" – Football Stories
Peckerhead!!

Anybody that knows me knows I have a very large tickle trunk full of Halloween costumes: from cows with udders; princesses and pirates; to completely inappropriate anatomically correct aprons – and everything in between.

I'm not sure where this one particular headpiece and accessory came from, but sometime in the last 20 years, I acquired a male appendage hat with a hairy testicles necklace.

One cold fall Bomber game, I arrived at the stadium and parked at the nearby hotel as usual. I got out of my car to put all my heavier clothing on and realized I had forgotten to bring a hat. It was around Halloween, which is probably why I had this headpiece and accessory in my car. I was thankful that I did, as that was the only thing I had to keep my head warm. Those were the days where I didn't have a lot of extra money to purchase a toque, but in hindsight…. Ya, ya, hindsight is 20/20, right?

I wore what I had and threw on the testicles necklace because if I'm going to walk around looking like a penis, I might as well look the entire part. The regular season ticket holders around us were making crude yet funny jokes about my hat. Let's face it, it's a penis hat – what did I expect, right?

At half time, Teresa and I went downstairs to get out of the wind when someone yelled out, "Hey, peckerhead!"

Well, *that* drew a crowd of gawkers! Someone started yelling an <u>action statement</u> that had to do with the necklace and then – next thing you know – there were a hundred people chanting the statement over and over. Teresa and I were stunned and not sure what to do, except to laugh.

Eventually the crowd lost interest but not before the fellow that sits behind us at the games, took a picture of Teresa and I folded into each other, laughing hysterically. It's a priceless photo we hold dear today.

I'm Speeding Because I Have To Poop!

Teresa and Shawna laughing while sporting anatomically correct headgear and necklace accessory

The "Grey Cup" To Beat

When Teresa and I made the decision to travel to Toronto and attend the 100th Grey Cup in November 2012, we had no idea how many blessings were going to be bestowed upon us.

Teresa had never used her travel royalty points she'd been collecting over the years until I mentioned paying for my air travel using mine that had accumulated. She looked up her balance and was pleasantly surprised that she also had enough points to pay for her return flight to Toronto. We went online and booked our air transportation. Perfect! One piece of the logistic puzzle solved, and a few more to go.

We needed to get Grey Cup game tickets and that wasn't easy. It was the 100th Grey Cup and tickets were very hard to come by as they were anticipating a sold out game.

I emailed Dave's cousin in Toronto and asked if the company he operated happened to have season tickets. If so, perhaps when Grey Cup tickets became available, he could grab an extra set for Teresa and me. While we waited for his cousin to get back to us, we started working on accommodations.

I surfed the web for <u>hotels near</u> the football stadium and a few popped up. I found the Intercontinental Hotel, located a block or two away from Rogers Centre and negotiated a smokin' hot deal for $150 per night. That's a steal in Toronto on any given day! Wow, what a find *that* turned out to be!

Connected to Convention Centre, where all the major parties were taking place and a short block away from Rogers Centre where Grey Cup was being played, this hotel was amazing! We could also see the CN Tower and the waterfront district from our hotel room. Simply stunning!

Outside the front doors of the hotel is where the street party took place with barricades blocking off traffic for a three-block radius. The main grandstand stage, located only feet away from the hotel entrance was super convenient. The beer gardens, restaurants, outside activities, and concerts were phenomenal and they took place right outside our hotel lobby doors.

The cherry on top is when we realized that we were in the same hotel that one of the Grey Cup teams was staying. We couldn't take an elevator or walk anywhere without running into a player or coaching staff. We had the opportunity to chat with the quarterback, his mom and son, and even got a photo with everyone.

Before and after the Grey Cup game, many players representing the CFL were in the lobby socializing with fans. As they say, "Location, location, location." This was a 10 out of 10!

Back to the tickets: After several months, Teresa and I got nervous as the tickets were released to the public. If we were going to buy tickets, we wanted to do it sooner, rather than later, to guarantee seats.

After I pestered Dave's cousin to let us know if he was able to secure tickets for us, he admitted that he had planned on giving us the tickets, so there was no need to purchase any through the ticketing agents. What? Really? We were blown away and most appreciative.

Airfare – check
Accommodations – check
Grey Cup tickets – check

Teresa's sister had acquired some beautiful soapstone carvings when she worked in Inuvik and Teresa picked out a gorgeous piece to give to Dave's cousin as a thank you for his generosity. As well, we bought him a nice meal and a couple of drinks to show our heartfelt appreciation.

Grey Cup festivities were crazy!

The free street festival included our Canadian Military. Several military personnel, along with combat vehicles were available for interactive experiences and photo opportunities. It also included interactive football activities and displays. We experienced some of the best food vendor carts and live concerts throughout the day. Even though the evenings were cool, it was warm enough to draw very large crowds each night.

We dropped by a restaurant after the CFL Alumni Luncheon was over and chatted with a few retired CFL players. I don't know what we were thinking but neither Teresa nor I brought a marker for signatures. Pictures were equally as memorable, so when we had the opportunity for a photo op with a player, we took it!

While we walked back from the alumni luncheon, we heard this guy trying to get our attention from across the street, yelling, "Hey, you got a marker?" We immediately recognized him as the former quarterback for Winnipeg, BC, Edmonton, and Hamilton, standing with a CFL fan. Unfortunately, we couldn't help this fan since we didn't have a marker for him. The retired quarterback crossed the street to chat with us and we capitalized on getting a quick photo of all of us.

This is how the entire weekend went. We chatted with CFL players in the hotel and in various venues throughout the downtown area. Even though I had come down with a bad head cold on Saturday night and was still feeling lousy the next day, Grey Cup Sunday was very exciting!

We wandered down to the area where TSN was set up, broadcasting live. Commentators were interviewing players, coaches, and panels of ex-CFL'ers. Everything was live and the energy was electric. I had a purple blinking hat that my colleague and friend David lent me for the event. I also wore it so, should we have gotten separated, Teresa would be able to find me in the crowd. At one point, we stood behind the commentator's chair and jumped up and down, making fools of ourselves. Hey, we got on TV and had our 15 seconds of fame!

We met up with Dave's cousin and his wife before the Grey Cup game and headed to the stadium together. We were very pleased with our tickets, which were on the 20-yard line about half way up the stands.

Rogers Centre is huge and the players still looked like salt and pepper, but we had a fabulous time enjoying the crowd and conversation with our hosts and people sitting around us.

At half time, Dave's cousin disappeared and returned just as the second half began. He asked us if we wanted to upgrade our seats as he had passes to a better section. That was a no-brainer! He gave us the passes on a lanyard that we would require to access the new seats. The seats were Box Seats located on the 45-yard line. At our disposal, we had access to free drinks, free food, and a pool table to play if we got bored. Again, we couldn't believe the awesome blessing that flowed our way this trip!

We had a choice of sitting in the open area by the food and pool table or to take a seat in one of three rows that were exclusive to the private box. Teresa and I took a seat in one of the rows, which also had a ledge in front of it for food and drinks.

My cold had started to get the best of me and the little energy I had was draining fast. I had no appetite or desire to engage in anything except water, but Dave's cousin insisted on getting me something from the bar. I ordered an ice-cold beer, thinking it would help my sore throat. I placed the tall stein of beer in front of me and enjoyed the game from these unbelievable seats. When I got up to let someone pass, my purse knocked the full beer over the edge, completely soaking the person's hair, jacket, and seat in front of me, then smashed onto the cement floor, splaying glass everywhere! I felt like such a fool, but it was an accident. I hadn't even had one sip of the beer yet! The people in front of me were not pleased and I apologized explaining it was my purse that had knocked it over. We did our best to clean it up but, to make matters worse, a girl walking around in sock feet ended up with two pieces of glass stuck in her foot.

After the game, we headed back to the hotel room as I had faded very quickly and needed to rest.

Dave's cousin had insisted that he pick us up the following day and drive us to the airport. I still felt awful the next morning and we packed up and waited for our ride to arrive. After waiting past the time he was supposed to arrive, he called to inform us that there was an accident on the main highway and that he couldn't make it after all. We needed to get a taxi immediately as we only had an hour and a half until our flight was boarding. While we had checked in online, we knew the lines would be long and security would be crazy! We were in trouble!

We explained our situation to the hotel doorman and he hailed a cab for us immediately. We told the cab driver when our flight was and he explained that there wasn't much hope in getting us there on time, *unless* we were prepared to close our eyes and experience the ride of our lives.

We replied, "Give'r! Let's go!"

To avoid the gnarly traffic on main roads, he took us through the residential areas at lightning speed, rounding corners on what felt like two wheels, weaving in and out of lanes and squeezing between traffic and parked cars. I love amusement rides and rollercoasters, but this guy rivaled every rock'n and roll'n ride I've been on. At times I think Teresa and I were half laughing and half crying, not quite certain if we were going to meet our maker or live to tell about this survival story in a Toronto cab.

We got to the airport with zero time to spare. The airline was calling our names over the intercom when we arrived and we immediately identified ourselves to an agent. She fast-tracked us through and notified the gate that we were on our way through security. The security line was long and there was no way we were getting through in time. We begged everyone to let us cut in front of the line and, in the end, we just made it on the plane before takeoff.

That Grey Cup absolutely, positively, and without a doubt, set the bar for all Grey Cups to come! Another fabulous trip with my BFF, Teresa!

Pace Yourself!

When I was young and foolish, my girlfriend Teresa and I went to Regina, Saskatchewan, on a Labour Day Classic football trip with a local tour bus company.

The Labour Day Classic is a match-up between the Winnipeg Blue Bombers and Saskatchewan Rough Riders. The Blue Bombers had a fairly decent team at the time, but the ratio of wins on Saskatchewan's turf was not in our favour.

When Dave dropped us off at the shopping centre to meet the bus, we very quickly realized that we were the oldest people on this crazy bus tour. While we waited to board the bus, Teresa and I sat on a curb strategizing how we were going to keep up with these youngsters.

"It's important that we pace ourselves," I said. "We have a cooler of assorted bevvies, but it needs to last until we get to Regina. If we're going to survive this bus trip with these children (aging from 18 to 25), we have to make it look like we're partaking with them, but we need to pace ourselves so that we still remain intact upon our arrival in Regina," I continued.

We agreed that this was a good plan. Teresa mentioned that she really didn't drink too much, especially first thing in the morning, and that she probably wouldn't even go through the bevvies she packed in the cooler.

In my estimation, this was likely going to be a very long and annoying road trip to Regina with these teenage party-hardy animals. It didn't take long before the party began and the bus was rockin'.

Teresa and I stayed in our groove until we passed Brandon, Manitoba, which is only two hours west of Winnipeg. We started interacting with the girls and guys on the bus by telling jokes and asking questions to one another. Marriage, children, work and, of course, football was discussed.

The cooler started to empty out a little quicker than we anticipated and decided it was a good time to crank the tunes!

"What bus driver? You don't have music to pipe through the speakers? "We'll just have to make some!" I exclaimed. My aunts used to sing and play harmonica around the fire at the lake and I got to know many interesting songs that you'd never hear on the radio. I taught these kids on the bus that you don't have to be young to be a little crazy, so I started singing these unique fire pit songs, which they loved.

"Sing us another one!" they shouted.

Teresa reminded me to pace myself as we still had a long way to go to Regina. She was one to talk as she made her way around the bus schmoozing (not smooching) with a couple of people she knew from her bowling league. Okay, I admit it. We weren't the only old farts on this tour, but darn close!

It was time to pull out the big guns and I started to sing a popular *country song, using* different lyrics. The bus erupted and everyone wanted to know the words to this song so, being the shy homegrown Mennonite girl I was, I did what was expected of me. I got on the bus microphone at the front of the bus and taught the entire bus how to sing this song. At one point, a large piece of cardboard was given to me so I could write the words on it to make it easier for everyone learn. Someone on the bus came up with the idea to sing it at the post-game party in the hotel hospitality room after the football game, and we did.

A couple hours outside of Regina, our cooler was empty and I was done! Falling asleep on the bus and feeling less than human upon our arrival to the hotel, Teresa was forced to check us in as I sat on our cooler in the lobby with my head plastered against a nice cool window.

I remember Teresa looking down at me after she checked us in and said, "This is why we agreed to pace ourselves, Shawna!"

I just nodded and closed my eyes again.

That night was a bit of a write-off as I had a headache a mile wide. However once that passed, it was all about football and fun. We all paced ourselves and enjoyed a fun-filled weekend!

Side note: After I arrived home, I noticed this massive bruise on my outer left thigh. I mean this thing was hu-mon-gous! I had no idea where it came from, so I called Teresa and asked her about it.

She burst out laughing and said, "Well, on the bus ride to Regina, you were sitting on the top of the headrest of your seat, balancing yourself while singing, and the driver turned a corner at which time you fell off the seat and landed on your side coming down hard on the armrest".

"Well, that explains it then," I said.

One more thing: Bombers won that game!!! Now you *know* that this took place a long time ago, as the Bombers haven't won a Labour Day game in Regina for many years.

Roar on the Shore

Knowing that Teresa and I experienced the most amazing Grey Cup ever, in Toronto, we knew that any Grey Cup celebration to follow could not be matched.

The Grey Cup game in Vancouver had quite the benchmark to live up to. Nonetheless, our expectations were high as we planned different events for the 2014 Grey Cup celebration in Vancouver.

I arrived a day before Teresa to spend time with my pseudo-brother, Blair. He's actually my second cousin, but since my brother passed away in 2010, we're more like siblings than cousins. Blair and I had a wonderful visit as he toured me through the downtown area before we settled in for a home-cooked lemon salmon pasta meal and a bottle of wine for some serious catch-up time.

It rained cats and dogs all evening and the forecast was for 100% chance of rain over the next three days. Great! Just great! Many of the free Grey Cup activities took place outside, but Blair told me that if people in Vancouver stayed in because of rain, the streets would be empty half the year. I was still disheartened about the weather as many of the events we wanted to take in were outdoors.

The next morning, it was cloudy but not rainy. Blair suggested that we meet Teresa at the airport so that she didn't get lost getting to his place. He suggested texting her to let her know that we would be greeting her at the airport, but I wanted to surprise her.

We arrived at her baggage carousel early and saw her come through the arrivals gate, heading to the washroom.

I ran up behind her, put my hands over her eyes and said, "Surprise!"

According to Teresa, she came close to knocking me on my arse, but quickly held back when she saw it was moi. I laughed it off and we headed to Blair's condo where our private accommodations were booked.

Blair lives in a condominium on the 11th floor. He pulled a few strings and rented us the guest suite for five nights on the 4th floor. It was absolutely perfect! It was private for us ladies, but still very close to visit with Blair on a moment's notice.

We settled into the guest suite, which consisted of a large room with a bed, huge closet, dresser, oversized chair, and TV. The bathroom was a good size for both of us to put our faces on in the morning together.

Blair's condo was within a 20-minute walk to any of the activities that were taking place in the downtown area. We simply couldn't have asked for a better location. The $50 per night guest room rental secured us the best deal in Vancouver on one of the most expensive weekends of the year.

We covered a lot of ground in the five and half days we were in Vancouver. Thankfully, the weather changed course and while it was cloudy for a couple days, we never saw any rain during the day. This allowed us to enjoy the activities at the outdoor street festival, as well as take in Vancouver's tourist attractions.

We checked out Granville Island and visited a microbrewery where we sampled some local beer. We also ate the best fish and chips in the Vancouver area, at a local fish stand. Seriously, you literally stood while you ate.

Teresa and I cooked Blair and his boyfriend Christian, a seafood dinner and played charades until the wee hours of the morning. Honest to goodness, I don't think I've ever seen Teresa laugh so hard. Her actions to describe "Stop, drop, and roll" sent us all to the floor laughing.

With the forecast advertising for a sunny day, we changed our plans and head to Grouse Mountain for a few hours. The transit system in Vancouver is bar-none, the best system I've ever experienced. We travelled by Canada-Line, Sea-bus, and regular transit to Grouse Mountain and the trip was worth the time. The gondola lift was not Teresa's favorite part, but once we were up at the top of Grouse Mountain, Teresa was amazed at the scenic views. Sadly, many of the attractions were closed and we couldn't fully appreciate all that Grouse Mountain had to offer. Dave and I had been there a couple years previous to this trip so I knew everything that Teresa was missing. She would have loved the grizzly bears that were already in part hibernation. The journey was a part of the experience and we had an incredible time.

We made it home in time to shower and prepare for the CFL Awards Ceremony, which took place a short, 10-minute walk from the condo.

We got dressed up and walked to the Queen Elizabeth Theatre where we were escorted into the building on a red carpet. We felt so special!

It's hard to describe the feeling of walking into an event that is intended to honour our CFL's greatest players. We chatted with many past and present players, coaches, commentators, and CFL franchise owners. Where possible, we also had pictures taken with them.

It was a wonderful evening and many great memories were made.

Since the forecast was calling for full sun, albeit a bit cool, we decided to make a full-day trip to Nanaimo on Vancouver Island and visit Marlene and Daryl, who are very good lake friends from Pinawa.

A year prior, Marlene and Daryl pulled up stakes in Manitoba and moved to Nanaimo to be closer to their daughter and three grandchildren.

Teresa had never been to Vancouver, so the Mountains and Pacific Ocean were a new experience for her.

We left early in the morning and arrived in Nanaimo around noon, where Marlene greeted us at the ferry terminal. After a tour of their apartment and the new house they were moving into the following week, we settled in for what seemed to be a quick visit over a glass of wine and the most amazing seafood clam chowder I've ever had. Since we wanted to take the 5pm ferry back to the mainland, our visit was a little shorter than we would have liked. After a big hug and one little tear, we were back on the ferry and headed to Vancouver!

The ferry ride home proved to be entertaining. We grabbed seats at the very front of the ferry facing the Nanaimo, thinking the ship would turn around when we were out on the ocean and we would be looking at the water, facing mainland. We learned that these ferries don't turn around, rather, they simply drive *into* port, and use a separate set of controls to drive *out* of the port. This meant that we had front row seats sitting backwards as the ship was heading to the mainland.

Since it was very dark and the ocean was pitch black, we could see our reflection quite clearly through the window. After we killed some time and looked around the on-board gift shop, we became bored and maybe even a little grumpy. The people beside us were very serious and didn't want to chat. They may have been tired and grumpy, too.

Time to perk things up!! I got out my smart phone and activated an app that takes pictures while distorting the object it's capturing. Teresa and I took many selfie pictures. After each picture, we reviewed each one to see how stupid we looked. Some of the pictures were so darn funny, we were crying and practically sliding off the seat laughing. We spent a good 20 minutes doing this until our stomachs hurt, our cheeks were sore, and any makeup that we had on, had long washed down our faces.

After acting like 12-year olds, we took a walk around the boat to stretch our legs. On our way back to the seats, a lady in the back row stopped and asked us if she could talk to us. I thought we were in trouble as we were making an awful lot of noise earlier. She told us that we had made her ferry trip a hilarious experience and she was so glad that she was on the same ferry as us. She had been feeling a little down and not looking forward to the hour and a half ride. We had made her laugh out loud and feel so much better. It was important to her that we knew what we had done for her. She explained that she didn't know exactly what we were doing, but she was sitting in the 4th row behind us and could see us in the reflection of the window howling with laughter. She continued to say that, at one point, she witnessed us almost slide off the seat. Teresa took it upon herself to explain what we were doing and then proceeded to show her the pictures. The lady had a good laugh and understood why we were having so much fun.

When we arrived home, we were tired and Teresa was a *weeeee* bit miserable. Originally, we planned to attend a Grey Cup social event, but sidelined that since we were both pretty pooped from our journey to the Island. Instead, we descended upon Blair's place, which cheered us up in less than 30 minutes. We played games, told stories, and laughed the night away.

The Grey Cup game was nothing short of amazing!

Our seats were five rows from the top, behind the goal posts, but honestly, the view was terrific anyways. We had arrived fairly early and had time to orientate ourselves with the stadium and our seats.

After a while, we got the smart phone out again and started taking funny pictures as well as goofy real-time photos, completely ignoring all of the staring eyes around us.

Most people who know me also know that I'm not very observant. Seriously, I could practically run over someone with my car before realizing that I know the person. I just don't look that close at people when I'm walking or driving. Something caught my eye, though. I saw someone I recognized walk up the stairs and stop about 4 rows in front of ours. Since we were sitting on the aisle, I shouted out to the person and she looked up. Unbelievable!! A former colleague Debbie Ledoux from Winnipeg also attending the Grey Cup was sitting in our section! What? That's crazy!! We snapped a few pictures to prove to our girlfriends back home that we ran into each other and then she re-joined her family to watch the game.

It's hard to compare the 100th Grey Cup in Toronto to the 102nd Grey Cup in Vancouver, as they were both very unique experiences. The accommodations in both Grey Cups had *everything* to do with the amazing time we had. I loved being so close to my bro/cousin Blair and saw him often.

Blair, thank you for being a huge part of our incredible trip and for hosting us ole' broads for five days. We loved every minute of it!!

Teresa had never been to the West Coast and to experience this trip through her eyes was a gift in itself.

I'm Speeding Because I Have To Poop!

Teresa chewing on Shawna's dreads at 102nd Grey Cup in Vancouver

Grey Cup '03 – BRING ON THE BANJOS!

Time for another road trip with my bestie, Teresa!

Instead of a bus tour, which reminded us that we really can't keep up with the 20-something babies, we drove to Regina in Teresa's SUV, sharing fuel and accommodation expenses. We both took Friday off and drove straight to Regina to begin our weekend of football and fun!

The Winnipeg Blue Bombers did not make it to the big game, but we were excited to watch the Edmonton Eskimos and the Montreal Alouettes duke it out for the second consecutive year. Losing the year prior, this was the redemption game for the Eskimos and they got it, winning the 91st Grey Cup by a 34/22 margin.

Just a couple months prior to the Grey Cup, a Bomber player made a politically incorrect statement to the press regarding our province to the West being inbred banjo pickers. He later gave a half-hearted apology and corrected himself by saying not all of them can play a banjo.

I, personally, was mortified and thought the comment was made in bad taste, even if it was made as a humourous overture.

Unfortunately, all the hotels were booked, which forced us to consider alternative options. One option was using the Homestay Program, where Regina residents opened up their homes to Grey Cup fans for $50 per night. After a successful application for this program, we were assigned to a home owned by a lovely lady...we'll call her Mary.

Upon our arrival, Mary showed us our accommodations in the basement of her home. It consisted of a 10x10 room, with an over-sized single bed for Teresa and me to share. It was also equipped with a small three-piece en-suite. Our accommodation was cozy, to say the least! Teresa and I slept together in this small bed, only spooning once or twice – just kidding. We slept together and it was tight, but it worked.

The evening of our arrival, Mary invited us upstairs for a glass of wine. Not wanting to offend her, we obliged before heading out to one of the parties near the stadium. We found out that she was a widow with no children. She went on to tell us that she had married her first cousin, which is why they never had children. This news challenged our every instinct to burst out laughing, as we silently reflected on the comment that our player had made earlier that season. We tilted our heads with a crooked smile and nodded, not knowing quite what to say. Regardless of what her story was, Mary was a perfect homestay host and we would stay there again, if the opportunity presented itself.

On Saturday, we headed to Riderville for a series of concerts featuring Doc Walker and Charlie Major. The free ride on the mechanical bull was tempting, but I chickened out last minute (bauck-bauck-bauck-bauck)! We danced and met a lot of people before grabbing a taxi back to Mary's house.

On Sunday, November 16, 2003, the Grey Cup game was cold but exciting. The Eskimo's won the Grey Cup and western Canadians were happy campers.

Teresa and I realized that there was no way we were going to be able to hail a cab immediately following the game, so we sauntered over to a bar close-by. It was a few short blocks away from the stadium and we only needed to kill an hour or so before traffic died down and a cab would be more easily available.

We ordered some nibbles and a drink and then called a cab. At that time, the taxi dispatcher indicated that there was a 30 to 45 minute wait. Neither of us was in a rush and continued to enjoy the live band that was playing in the bar.

After around 30 minutes, we paid our tab and waited outside for the taxi. We waited and waited and waited and waited. After 30 minutes, we called the taxi company again but the line rang busy, even after repeatedly calling.

It was approaching 10pm by now and we were tired and looking worn out from being outside all day, but we didn't have a car and the taxis weren't available. We finally got through to the taxi dispatch and were told that the taxi would be another hour. Knowing that there was nothing we could do, we retreated back into the bar and ordered more bar food and another drink while we waited. The band was excellent, but after their last set and still no taxi coming our way, we knew we were in trouble.

We called the cab company AGAIN and when we finally got through, they indicated that a cab was on the way. Not wanting to miss the cab, we waited outside for it this time. We waited and waited and waited.

Eventually the band started to load their equipment in the van and noticed that we were outside getting cold. We explained that we had been waiting for three hours for various cabs that never showed up. They took pity on us and offered us a ride back to Mary's place. It turns out that one of the band members lived a couple blocks away from her house. We were most appreciative and grateful that these strangers would give us a ride home.

Now, I know what some of you readers might be thinking! Don't *ever* take a ride with strangers, right? I would normally agree with you, except we were cold and desperate. Period. That's our only excuse. We were fine and we were together.

This Grey Cup experience allowed us to fully appreciate the hospitality from the fine folks in Saskatchewan. Thank you Regina – we had a blast!!

Chapter V

More Of My Fabulous Friends And Family

I Know They're Here Somewhere!

I went to my colleague Vaughn Simpson's place to look at some used furniture he was selling. When I arrived, I parked out front and checked out his brand new boat in the driveway before heading into the house. Vaughn gave me a quick tour of his place and then escorted me to the garage to check out two leather chairs I was interested in. Vaughn had recently downsized to a smaller home and all excess furniture and electronics were being stored in the garage.

The chairs were buried deep inside the garage behind kitchen, bathroom, bedroom, and living room furniture. We had to move literally every piece of furniture in order to access the chairs, which I of course wanted to see in the daylight. Most of the furniture had to be pulled out of the garage and put on the lawn in order to get to the chairs. Once they were outside, I made sure they were comfortable and measured them to ensure they would fit in our screen room at the lake.

"Yup...I'll take them!" I said.

Vaughn suggested that I bring my truck around the back where I could load the chairs much easier, but when I got to my truck, my keys were nowhere to be found.

I looked underneath the truck (thinking maybe I dropped them). Nope, not there! "I'll check the boat," I said to myself, thinking maybe I dropped them in there while looking at it earlier. Nope... not there either!

Scrambling to remember where I had been in Vaughn's place, I thought perhaps I dropped them when touring the house. After retracing my steps through the house, I still came up empty!

After Vaughn put most of the furniture back in the garage, he came looking for me and wondered what was keeping me.

I explained that I had I misplaced my keys and had already searched around my truck, in his boat, and in his house.

"Oh no, I bet they are somewhere in the garage!" Vaughn said.

Vaughn and I moved around every single piece of furniture in the garage thinking that perhaps I had them in my hand and dropped them while trying to access the chairs. After 20 minutes of searching the garage, we again came up empty.

At this point, I was getting mad.

Vaughn had just moved into this house and the people who owned the home before him had not taken care of the yard or shrubs around the deck. Everything was overgrown, thorny, and prickly. You couldn't see anything through the dead leaf accumulation and weeds in the flowerbeds and grass.

The only other option was that I had them in my hand and dropped them in the yard while taking out the furniture from the garage. "GREAT... I'll never find them in this yard," I thought. Never the less, I had to try.

I started to pick out all the dead leaves in the shrubs to see if they had fallen out of my hands and said to myself, "Ah, screw it!"

I promptly started pulling out all the shrubs and perennial bedding plants from the overgrown area and tossing them in the yard.

Vaughn just stared at me and said, "Shawna, what the heck are you doing?"

"They're dead anyways," I replied, "I'm actually doing you a favour and saving you money on a gardener!" Vaughn stood there shaking his head and wondered if his colleague had lost her ever-loving mind!

After I weeded his shrubs at yet another unsuccessful attempt to locate my keys, I got down on my hands and knees and started with the grass. I patted down every square in of grass that I had been on that afternoon. I got pricked by thorns and started cursing (I may have started earlier. In fact, I'm pretty sure I did… maybe even right after we searched the garage).

After an hour-long search, I resigned myself to the fact that I had lost my entire set of keys somewhere on Vaughn's property and was not going to find them that day. I called Dave to ask him to bring me another set of keys and he encouraged me to give it one more try. If I hadn't found them in 15 minutes, I was to call him back and he would bring me the spare set.

Vaughn checked the side-yard thinking maybe I dropped them by the side-gate while I continued to pat down the grass one more time.

I was getting a little emotional and needed a tissue. Still on my hands and knees, I sat up a bit and glanced down as I reached into my pocket. That's when I made the discovery!

"Vaughn, I found them!" I shouted.

Vaughn walked over, "Where?"

I reached down and pulled them out of my bra!!

His jaw dropped as he stared at me. "Are you shittin' me?"

I knew I had them in my hands when we started to move furniture around. At some point, I must have needed both my hands and shoved them in my cleavage so I wouldn't lose them!

For those of you who don't know the size of keychain that I have, allow me to enlighten you. It's the size of a fist. It has 12 different keys including house, trailer, car, truck, lake shed, home shed, work, my folk's house, and Dave's mom's house. Like most newer cars, my car key alone is a medium-sized fob.

It is hard to comprehend how I did not feel them while I stretched and bent in many different positions when moving furniture around the garage and hauling many pieces outside. They were nestled perfectly far enough down where I couldn't see them nor feel them. Had I not seen that little glimmer of metal when reaching for my tissue, I would have lost them until I took my clothes off that night!

Back to the story!!

As I dialed Dave's phone number for the final time that day, Vaughn said, "Give me the phone Shawna." Dave answered and all I heard was Vaughn's part of the conversation.

"Hi Dave, it's Vaughn… *pause*…Good, how are you…*pause*…Ya, she found them so you don't need to bring another set… *pause*…In her bra!… *pause*…..Nope, I'm not kidding! Say, you're not missing any boat motors or power tools that I need to ask her about are you?"

I laughed and cried while a mini-meltdown unfolded on Vaughn's prickly grass. I felt so stupid but relieved that the keys were located.

When Vaughn got off the phone, he emphatically stated, "So, you *know* that I'm going to tell this story to everyone at the office on Monday, right?"

I simply nodded.

Vaughn did indeed tell the story on Monday morning.

Now whenever we can't find a 3-hole punch or large office supplies at the office, people say, "Check with Shawna – she might have it stuffed between the girls!"

It's a story that will go down in history at work and has been repeated many times to new employees and guests.

Oh, and by the way, I ended up changing my mind and never bought the chairs. While I lost my dignity that day, Vaughn lost the sale of the chairs and most of his bedding plants and shrubs! I still feel terrible about that.

A little clarification from Vaughn: *While Shawna may remember my yard as a desolate wasteland; in fact, it was once a beautiful oasis of lush green grass, beautiful flowers, and well-manicured flower beds. It BECAME a wasteland, post-Shawna… and she didn't even buy the chairs after all that. Hmmmmph. *kick**

Rebuttal from Shawna: *Ya right buddy! I should of taken pictures! I did buy you a package of flower seeds to replace the dead ones I kindly removed for you - LOL*

A Moon For June

When my brother Vince moved from Calgary to Winnipeg, us sisters, Nancy, June, and I piled into Dave's truck to help him move home.

We arrived on a Saturday afternoon, packed the vehicles, and started home Sunday morning, less than 24 hours after arriving in Calgary.

Vince had a car so the return trip was made in two vehicles. Nancy and I drove in the truck while June and Vince drove his car.

On the way back to Winnipeg, with little sleep and growing tired of driving, I got cranky. June and Vince hatched a plot to pick up my spirits and create some fun back in the trip. While we were on a 4-lane stretch on the Trans-Canada Highway, Vince passed me while June hung a moon out the window. Nancy was very quick to grab a 33mm camera in the truck and took a picture of her hanging a moon. A hard copy of the picture was later given to June and Nancy kept a copy for herself. We knew that someday we would pull this picture out of the archive and use it for a milestone birthday gag. June said that if that picture ever surfaced that she would lie through her teeth and tell people that she had just had wisdom teeth surgery and her face was swollen! She said she'd never admit that it was her arse hanging out the window.

Warp speed ahead to June's 50th birthday.

Since June lived in Penticton, BC, at the time she was turning 50, Nancy and I organized a birthday party to take place in Calgary at Nancy and Jim's place.

I flew down from Winnipeg and June and Barry drove in from Penticton. My cousin Pearl as well as Dave's brother, Harvey, and his fiancée, Sunny D, also attended the party.

Nancy and I made her a card and my responsibility was a poem and some pictures. The rest would be completed when I arrived in Calgary. Nancy looked high and low for the picture of June's moon from the 1990's but couldn't find it. We asked my niece Robyn (June's daughter) if she had the photo as June asked Robyn to store a lot of her photographs that she hadn't moved yet. Nope, Robyn couldn't find it either. So I did what all good sisters would do in a time of desperation, and re-created the scene of the crime.

I called up my friend and said, "Joanie, I need your help if you're interested and available."

"Of course! What's up?" Joanie replied.

I explained that Nancy and I were making a special card for June's 50th birthday and that I needed to recreate a picture of a moon being hung outside of a car on a highway. Honest to goodness, I'll never forget her response for as long as I live.

"Shawna, I love you and would do almost anything for you, but I'm not hanging my ass out the window so you can take a picture of it!"

I burst out laughing and assured her that it wouldn't be her arse, but rather mine. Her only deed would be to take the picture. She enthusiastically agreed!! This was getting very up close and personal with a friend, but Joanie was super pumped to be a part of a Derksen experience.

I picked Joanie up that day and we headed to the south Perimeter Highway where I parked the car along the service road, facing west. After getting the right camera angle to make it look like we were on the highway, I perched myself inside the vehicle, hanging my bare butt outside the window while wiggling my pants down around my ankles and balancing over a gearshift; all the while, laughing so hard I could barely keep my balance. Seriously, tears were running down my face as I'm yelling at Joanie to "hurry up"!

Honestly, I can't believe I was doing this for a birthday card!

In the middle of the shoot, Joanie noticed a guy walking his dog in the field just behind her on the service road. We're not sure if he saw anything, but we laughed at the idea that maybe he did and he likely wondered what in the sam-blazes was going on. Oh well... good entertainment for him if he did!

Joanie got a couple of great shots and it actually looked like the original picture. Other than the fact that my car is 20 years newer and my sister's butt is 20 times smaller than mine, it was a really good re-creation of that picture.

Before, during and after the photo shoot, Joanie and I laughed so hard. She couldn't believe she had taken a picture of my butt in broad daylight on a busy highway. Yes, our friendship was launched to a whole new level!

We used that picture on June's 50th birthday card and even incorporated it into her birthday poem (which you read earlier in her section of the book). When June first saw the picture, she thought we found the old photograph, but the poem gives the story away and she eventually realized that it was a recreation. I seriously considered putting that picture in this book but decided to let the readers use their imaginations instead. Smart move Peterson!

Jeff! Long Time, No See!

When Teresa and I had season tickets to the Winnipeg Blue Bombers, we sat in a super fun section with some regular season ticket holders that held the same seats for 25 plus years.

Billy, the primary season ticket holder sat directly behind us. He would alternate the seat beside him with his buddies Al and Jeff. As a result, we got to know all three of them quite well over the years.

There were seasons where Jeff would attend most of the games and other times when Al would be there. Every now and again, after the football game, we would go to a nearby bar and celebrate the Blue Bomber's victory.

Suffice to say, we got to know these three well and enjoyed watching the Bomber games with them.

Changing gears and bringing this story up to date:

I was at work and needed a break. The downtown mall was close to work, so I trotted down there for 20 minutes of peace and quiet.

I sat down with my cup of coffee, enjoying my newspaper when I saw Jeff sitting there by himself.

I grabbed my coffee and walked up to his table and said, "Hi there!"

Very friendly, he replied, "Hi, how are you?"

I sat down and we carried on a conversation of pleasantries for a couple minutes. I mentioned to him that he hadn't been at the football games lately and he acknowledged that he'd been busy and not able to make it to many this year.

At this time, his food order arrived and it looked delicious. I looked over at his waffles, blanketed in strawberries and whip cream and almost dug my fork into it for a little bite when he gave me the strangest look.

At first I thought to myself, "He doesn't want you to have a bite Shawna. Leave it alone."

Then another thought crept up on me. It was not only in the look he gave me but something seemed off so I said, "You're not Jeff are you?"

"Nope, I'm not," he replied.

"Why didn't you say so?" I countered back. "We've been chatting for five minutes and all the time I thought you were the guy, Jeff, who sits behind me at Bomber games."

He didn't quite know how to respond, except to say that during our conversation he was trying to figure out who I was and where he might have known me. Everyone has those moments in life where someone knows *you* yet you cannot come up with where you might know *them*. He simply had drawn a blank – and rightfully so! He explained that he did go to a lot of football games and assumed that's where I knew him. When we compared seat sections, they were on opposite sides of the stadium. It was a sheer coincidence we were able to carry on a conversation for several minutes about the Bombers without figuring out that he wasn't who I thought he was. I told him that he had a twin in Winnipeg who also goes to the Bomber games.

It wasn't worth trying to save my pride, so I didn't bother. Instead I apologized for disturbing his breakfast, not to mention almost helping myself to it, and then promptly returned to work.

I sat in my workstation and laughed periodically throughout the day, wondering what this guy must have been thinking. I can only imagine the story that he told when he returned to work or home that day!

"I'm minding my own business after a long midnight shift and some blonde chick came up to me while I was having breakfast and almost helped herself to it and starting chatting me up, blah blah…"

I told that story to Billy and Jeff, who were both at the next Bomber game and we all had a good laugh about it.

Kathleen McCarthy

As promised, the endless, hilarious moments we shared shall remain between us. I love you to pieces my friend!!

My good friend, Kathleen McCarthy

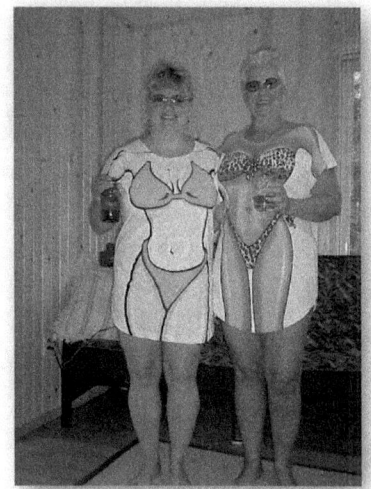

**Shawna and Kathy:
This is what we REALLY
look like under all
our clothes**

Got Salt?

In 1999, Dave and I arrived in Pinawa with an older fifth wheel trailer that we purchased from my folks.

That year, on a hot summer day, I was floating on my canvas air mattress with a string tied to the buoy rope that sectioned off the swimming area. The Winnipeg River had quite a strong current and I didn't want the air mattress and I to float away, so tying it to the buoy rope was an awesome solution.

In the distance, I saw someone paddling towards me on a canvas air mattress just like mine. I was pleased when this lady came up to the ropes and started to chat with me. She introduced herself as Marlene, and we chatted for over an hour. After we were finished in the sun, she invited me back to her place for a refreshment to continue our visit.

Since we were tied to the swimming area perimeter ropes/buoys and I was currently on the outside of the ropes, I needed to get the inside before paddling back to the beach. While staying on the air mattress, I first tried going under the ropes/buoys. When that didn't work, I tried going over the ropes/buoys but that didn't work either.

"I'm going to have to get off my mattress and swim under the rope while throwing it over the rope," I said to Marlene. Hopefully, I could do this without the current taking me down stream.

Acting quickly, I dove under water to get to the inside of the swimming area. The current must have been stronger than I thought as I got caught up in the buoy rope. I came up with the buoy rope chaffing the inside of my leg with the string on my air mattress twisted around both the rope and myself.

"Eeek! The rope is slimy and gross," I shouted.

Eventually, I got myself untangled and both the mattress and I got to shore safely.

I had brought our truck to the beach and parked it in an odd direction. Dave had already walked back to the site, so I had to turn it around to get it in the direction of Marlene's site. I backed up the truck and tried to straighten it out. When I pulled it forward to turn the hood of the truck in the proper direction, I landed up in the ditch between the beach and the road. Thankfully, some strong guys on the beach noticed the dilemma and pushed the truck out.

We finally got to Marlene's site and I felt something weird between my legs. I looked down and saw several small leeches on my inner thigh. I screamed and started to freak out. Marlene quickly ran to their picnic table and got a saltshaker. Marlene added to my stress when she informed me that I had many leeches in that vicinity. The last thing I wanted was for this nice lady, whom I had just met, to have to examine my privates and tell me where those suckers (literally) were, but that's exactly what I had to do.

"Marlene, can you check to see if there are any on the backs of my legs near my butt?" I requested.

"Oh my goodness Shawna, there are leeches back there too," she replied, as she grabbed the saltshaker from my hands. I bent down for her to apply the salt and she then said, "Shawna, you have 2 huge leeches on your ass!"

I screeched and danced around her site like I was avoiding a swarm of bees, completely freaked out!

"Lay over the picnic table and I'll pour salt all over them," Marlene commanded.

I did as I was told and breathed long and deep breaths as I tried not to think about the suckers on my cheeks. All I felt was the peppering of salt on my arse and then a little pinch as Marlene picked and flicked them off.

Meanwhile, Daryl, Marlene's husband, whom I had not yet met, had just woken up from an afternoon nap. I might have been the cause of that with all the screaming. As he looked out the window, he saw his wife shaking salt over a someone's bare butt as the stranger laid spread eagle, face down on their picnic table. Instead of attempting to help or ask for an explanation, he simply watched and chuckled.

At first when Marlene had de-leeched me, I felt awkward, as I hadn't known this woman for two hours before she was forced to get an up close and personal look at my crotch and butt. After the shock wore off, which didn't take too long, we both laughed, cracked open a beverage, and toasted to our newfound friendship!

This was the start of a long-standing friendship, which I treasure to this day!

Daryl and Marlene Michaluk

Shawna J Peterson

Farewell to Marlene and Daryl
(Written by Shawna and Carole Dupuis)

Daryl and Marlene
Near and dear to our heart
We all met in Pinawa
Who knew what THAT would start!

Many laughs around the fire
Swimming and jumping off the dock
Smokin' Saturdays and Murder Mystery Nights
Those things and more have made our friendship rock!

We said, "let's all meet in Mexico"
"And have fun in the sun and sand"
Bucerias and Guayabitos was where
We ate, drank and tanned!

Our memories will last forever
Never will they die
True friends stay together
And never say goodbye!

Daryl's - 62nd Birthday
(Written by Shawna and Pat McBride)

Happy birthday dear Daryl
Happy birthday ole friend
Since it's September
It's "that time" again

It's hard I believe
That you caught up to Pat
You're 62 now?
But still a great catch

Your Nissan, your TV
Your rum and your wine
You enjoy all these things
To have a good time

Age over 60
Is not over the hill
It's just near the top
So relax…. Take a pill

You're only as old
As the woman you feel
So grab the cute broad you married
And hang her your eel

Shawna J Peterson

Larry & Llowyin's - 40th Wedding Anniversary
(Written by Shawna)

Here stands Llowyin and Larry
For 40 Years they've been married
Through thick and thin
Through righteous and sin
Their love alone has carried

That's all for being sentimental
No more shall I be gentle
Let me share my truth
It'll have no couth
And I might sound a trite quite mental

Where shall I start to describe these two?
They are the same and yet so different
They both love their wine
Extravagant they dine
Larry's cuisine is so magnificent

Llowyin has, more patience than Job
Of this I know I'm sure
For when Ted and Larry
Have their male bonding time…it's scary
And it's more than most wives could endure

But Llowyin sticks by her main man
So we know, it must be love alone

I'm Speeding Because I Have To Poop!

For Larry is the love of her life
The one that completes her home

Now onto Larry, the ever-so-witty charmer
He's a hard man not to love
His humour is infectious
His cooking is incredulous
He always goes "over and above"

He's helpful and handy
And without a doubt
Would give you the shirt off his back
The only catch is, he may say "you first"
Anything, to see "a rack"

With beer in one hand
And a tool in the other
Larry loves his time at the lake
With projects and hobbies with his dear brother Ted
Nothing can stand in his wake

And who could forget the soft gentle voice
As Larry sings around the fire
When he sings, everyone listens
Except, Merle…who joins in an octave higher

Their children are a source of pride
And the "in-laws" are precious too
The time with their grandkids
Is sacred and special
It's more than what many grandparents do

Now these are my thoughts
Of Larry and Llowyin
You may see a totally different side
We're celebrating their marriage
Of 40 amazing years
I'll bet it was one heck of a ride!!

Larry & Llowyin's - 50th Wedding Anniversary
To the tune of "The Flintstones"
(Written by Shawna)

Wes'-lakes, meet the Wes'-lakes
There a cool and friend-ly fa-m-i-ly
To-day, they will cel-e-brate
Their 50th Wedding An-ni-ver-sa-ry

With their, friends and family by their side
They will, party till the sun starts to rise

Wes'-lake's, may your love grow
With some more yaba-daba-doo time
A bit of "foo-foo" time
For a-nother 50 years!!

I'm Speeding Because I Have To Poop!

Ode To My Friend
(And Her Legendary Farts)
(Written by Shawna)

T'was the night before Christmas
And all through the trailer
Was fartin' and tootin'
Like a New England Sailor

Her gas was so bad
Hubby almost moved out
Then he had an idea
He'd close that old spout

He tried with a cork
And even a candle
But when she let loose
It was more than he could handle

With needle and thread
He found in her sewing basket
He needed to do this
Or risk ending up in a casket

So under the covers
Ole hubby did crawl
Oh nuts…she let out another one
And he started to bawl

She wiggled and jiggled
And wouldn't stay still
But mission accomplished!!
He closed down the ole mill

Shawna J Peterson

She thought she was dreamin'
But when she awoke
Her horn-hole was sealed
This was no joke!

"How shall I poop?"
She says to her pal
I don't really care
At least there will be no smell

I'm Speeding Because I Have To Poop!

Girlfriend's 60'ish Birthday
(Written by Shawna)

Happy birthday buddy
Happy birthday dear friend
You know you're getting older
When your farts come out from all ends

Sometimes it's a "left cheek sneak"
And at times, it creeps out from the right
But the ones that come out straight up between the cheeks
Are usually, explosions of dynamite

It's hard to hold our farts inside
And frankly, it's not a natural or healthy thing
So let'er rip, just try not to s*#t
As a "shart" is far more embarrassing

We push and lean to get those suckers out
As our tummy's are full of gas
If others don't like it, well too frickin' bad
They can darn well, kiss our a$$

I want you to note that I haven't mentioned your age
At all in this poem just yet
I'll keep it a secret as long as I can
But "next year's" is one that no-one will forget

Shawna J Peterson

Suzy-Q
(When Her Retina Detached)
(Written by Shawna)

Roses are red
Violets are blue
I pray that Sue's eye
Will be as good as new

Once it's all healed
And she can see again
She'll be back to her ole self
Without any pain

I'm sorry you're hurting
And feel a bit scared
Please believe this will get better
And that so many people do care

I'm Speeding Because I Have To Poop!

Suzy-Q
(Returning To Work After Eye Surgery)
(Written by Shawna)

There lives a girl name Sue
Whose retina detached, that's true!
With "so-so" vision
But her spirits arisen
And a perfectly working "foo-foo"!

I missed her so much
At work and such
Our talks about sexy stuff to start
Her beautiful eyes
With a million dollar smile
Along with her amazing heart

She's back at work
And full of energy and perk
I for one am elate
Not only did my colleague return
So did my friend, my bud and my mate

Vegas Unleashed

Seriously, I don't even know where to start with this story. From the moment I got into my girlfriend Pat's car, until the day we returned home, we did not stop laughing. Have you ever had one of those trips where everything just worked out? Where all the planets align and nothing went wrong? Well, that's how I would summarize this trip, however Pat may see it a little differently.

Pat and I have never travelled together. In fact, I only knew Pat through her sister, Marlene (the same one who picked leeches off my butt). The idea to travel to Vegas with Pat started in a car dealership while I was waiting for my car to be serviced. I surfed the web for airfares to Las Vegas and found a deal of the century! The total trip including taxes, airfare, accommodations, and ground transportation between the airport and hotel was $341. The catch was that it was a last-minute holiday, which needed to be taken in a two-week period. This was too good of a deal to pass up.

I called Dave and asked if I could go. "Please baby, it's so cold and I can't wait until March when we leave for Mexico. I'm miserable and need a break from these Siberian temperatures."

Of course, Dave being Dave said, "Book it and have fun."

I really need to give full props to Dave since the time I would be away would be the same time he was working up north in minus-million temperatures. I also emailed my boss and got permission to take a few days off. I now had the permission from the two people I needed and had to put my thinking cap on to figure out whom to go with.

Like me, most of my friends are also working and can't take time off on short notice. I knew I wanted to go with someone fun who had a flexible work schedule. Admittedly, I tried a couple of close friends first. When those people weren't available, I thought of Pat, whom I've had a lot of fun with at the lake on the few occasions I've seen her. I didn't know Pat well but what I did know, I liked! Since she runs her own business, she also has flexibility with her work schedule.

I texted Pat and asked her if she was interested in going to Las Vegas.

Her response was, "Who is this?"

When I identified myself via text, she responded, "Are you serious about Vegas?"

Instead of continuing the conversation through a text, I called her and asked if she was interested in taking advantage of a cheap trip to Las Vegas. She agreed to go without thinking twice. The only glitch was that she was leaving for Jamaica the next day and would only be home a couple days before we would be scheduled to leave for Vegas. There was no time to waste and we would need to book this trip today…ASAP!

As soon as my car was ready, I headed straight to her place to get this trip booked. Within 45 minutes, I was at her door and we were online in search of the same deal I had found earlier.

After an hour and a half of technical glitches on the travel website, we called the agency instead. Finally, we were booked for four days and three nights at the hotel located in the middle of the Las Vegas strip. S-E-WEEEET!!!

Pat picked me up at work in minus-bazillion temperature for the 100th day in a row. Okay, it was probably minus 35 Celsius for the 45th day in a row, but after a couple of weeks in those frigid temperatures, it didn't matter…it was just plain cold…again! We lived in eternal Siberia that year and I was elated to be getting out of Winnipeg.

On our way to the airport, I thought it was only fair to warn Pat of one of my less than flattering habits: I was gassy. Yep, I'm a farter. They rarely stink, they are usually loud and I always own up to it. In fact, thanks to my girlfriend Joanie, I actually celebrate them by saying "Olé"! I think it was Joanie's way of excusing herself for farting, but somewhere along the way I adopted this saying and have even put the hand-motions in affect by circling my pointer finger in the air above my head while saying "Olé!" each time I fart. Anyways, Pat had been warned and accepted the challenge. We decided that our trip would be considered a complete success if one of us ended up in the back of a police cruiser. Of course we were kidding, but the wheels in our heads had begun to spin. Our laughter-filled holiday had officially begun!

After a nice lunch in the Winnipeg Airport, it was time to head to the security gate. The line was long, so I suggested to Pat that we could fast track the lineup by offering to have our hands swabbed for illegal substances at the security point. Of course, both our tests were negative and we moved through security quickly.

By the time we got on the plane, we were completely sober drunks who laughed at everything, whether it was funny or not. My tummy was making some noises and I immediately knew the cause. We had finished a big lunch and the meal was starting to digest. Yes, I needed to fart. So, leaning slightly to the right, I let out a "left cheek sneak". Planes are loud so it doesn't really matter, as nobody can hear; however, this one was not a normal fart. It was quiet and I hadn't done the "Olé" motion, so I thought I'd gotten away with one. Wrong! The term silent and deadly was right on the money!

My nose started to twitch and I knew I had to warn Pat. I tapped her on the shoulder and before I could say, "Olé! Sorry, this one was a stinker," she turned to look at me, her eyes went wide, and then rolled towards the window. Her mouth slightly curled and a look of horror that confirmed what I had suspected. This one reeked! I didn't ever get the opportunity to say "Olé" or warn her. No words were required. We shook in our seats, laughing ourselves to tears.

Our arrival in Las Vegas was interesting, as we couldn't figure out which shuttle stop to wait for our bus at. Dragging our luggage from one end of the airport to the other, we eventually found the right pick-up area and boarded our shuttle.

A group of young men, who had clearly started their holiday on the plane, started calling us Birdies (as in "old birds", I assumed). As they made comments from the back of the bus, one of them moved to a seat behind us and initiated a conversation. Apparently, they were in Vegas for a concrete convention, which Pat and I assumed was a code word for a bad boy's weekend. One young man in particular took an interest in Pat and was trying to make time with her.

They chatted with us and asked if we wanted to party with them, to which we replied, "Thanks, but our children are older than you."

The shuttle dropped them off at their hotel and we proceeded onto ours thinking that these two old birds still got it!

With not a soul in the reception line, we were able to check in and score a moderate room upgrade. We were pleasantly surprised by the size of the room, even if the furniture was straight out of the 1980's. Both beds were comfortable and we knew we would only be in the room to sleep, so the decor truly didn't matter. The accommodation was more than adequate.

Remember, this is all for $341: flight, accommodation, transfers, and taxes.

Throughout the entire holiday, we had both adopted the routine of saying "Olé," complete with the circular hand and pointed finger motion in the air after each fart. It's only fair to say that I wasn't the only one who farted either! We laughed every time. It didn't matter where or when. As long as the farts were being released, "Olé" immediately followed!

I'm a very social person and while we would walk The Strip, we'd stop and talk to people. Many would ask if we planned to see any shows while in Vegas.

I would reply, "Yes, one special show for my friend here. It's called *Menopause*."

That's kind of ironic now since as I write this book, I'm in full-blown menopause!

Pat would call me a nasty name and then let out a loud laugh to follow. Nothing was taken personally, but there were a couple times that I might have gone too far.

After a long walk along The Strip, we headed back to the hotel at a faster pace than usual. Pat had to use the washroom very badly. You know it's not #1, right? She wanted to crap in her own litter box and didn't want to stop at one of the 10 casino washrooms we passed along the way. We barely made it up to the room before Queenie commanded the washroom as her personal throne!

"That was close. Another minute or so and I would have shit my pants," Pat confessed.

I tucked that little incident into the back of my mind for future reference!

I'm normally not like this, but something was different about this trip. It was like I was "unleashed" or something.

The next day, we walked over to grab a 99-cent High-Boy Miller beer at a small gift shop near the hotel. Where on earth can you buy a beer for 99 cents, never mind in a tall-can?

"Well, well, well, what do we have here?" I asked Pat.

Parked right beside the store was a police cruiser with a hunky officer sitting in the front seat. Immediately, Pat and I started to plan how one of us was going to get into that back seat. All we needed was enough time for the other to take a picture of one of us back there.

We casually walked up to the officer and started to chitchat with him. We started off with light conversation about where we were from and what brought us to Vegas. We also talked about how bizarre it was to be able to buy a beer so cheap and enjoy it while walking The Strip. In Canada, this would be illegal and you could get arrested for that.

I casually took a look in the back seat of the car and pointed out that the seats were molded plastic, which I had never seen before. The officer replied that the seats are not meant for comfort and went on to explain that, sometimes, bodily fluids are smeared over the back. Molded plastic was easier to clean than material. Pat jumped in on the conversation and added that the fluids probably included, puke, pee, and blood. The officer completed the list by saying that often people poop themselves in the back seat as well.

I didn't know what I was saying until it was out of my mouth, I swear!

"Oh, just like you almost did yesterday, Pat!" I said with a smirk on my face that indicated I knew I was a completely dead woman.

Pat called me another nasty name in front of the kind officer and walked away, with her head down, shaking it from side-to-side and laughing. When I caught up to Pat, we were laughing so hard that we could barely stand. That was our best opportunity to get into the back of a cruiser and she abandoned the mission!

The next morning, Pat kept rubbing her back on the door jam and walls in the hotel room.

I asked, "Pat, what the heck are you doing?"

"I'm trying to rub off the friggin' target you've put on my back!" she replied, using her dry, stoic, humourous voice.

For a moment, I felt bad; but just for a moment.

Pat and I toured a few places that we agreed upon earlier in the trip:

1. Old Vegas on Freemont Street
2. The Premier Outlet Shopping Mall
3. The Gold and Silver Shop (Pawn Stars show)
4. Count Customs (Counting Cars show).

While this shopping trip was not as successful as my previous trips to Las Vegas, we managed to find a few good deals along the way.

On the way back, the taxi driver dropped us off at Count Customs, which specializes in high-end, expensive custom engine and bodywork on old vehicles. I've often watched the show *Counting Cars* with Dave, and the cast members of the show are the actual people who work in the shop. While we didn't see Danny, the shop owner, we saw a couple of the employees working on vehicles and walking through the showroom, which was open to the public. It was a really neat experience.

While we were waiting for our taxi to arrive, we noticed a restored bus that is owned by Horny Mike, one of the *Counting Cars* employees and actors. Horny Mike has spiky hair and helmets that are made of horns or spikes. The showroom actually has a display of all his helmets and headpieces, which are very cool.

We walked over to Horny Mike's restored bus and started taking pictures. Pat suggested that I stand in front of the bus while she took a picture of me. As I was posing in front of the bus, this guy comes running up the parking lot and jumps into the picture, placing an arm around me. It turns out to be Horny Mike himself! Very cool! We chatted for a few minutes before he had to return to the shop.

Horny Mike suggested that we use their limo service to return to our hotel and since we had waited so long for a taxi that clearly wasn't coming, we accepted.

When Sam, our limo driver, picked us up, there were a couple of guys waiting for a taxi as well. They asked us if we would share our limo with them. Their hotel was just a couple blocks before ours, so we agreed to share Sam with them.

We had no idea how much a limo ride was going to cost and being in Vegas, we knew it wouldn't be cheap. Since there were four of us splitting the limo costs, it was likely going to be less costly than Pat and I taking a cab back to our hotel ourselves.

No sooner after pulling out of the parking lot, we heard the guy in the front seat (one of the guys that we agreed to share our limo with) negotiating a ride to downtown Vegas so him and his buddy could visit the Silver and Gold Shop where *Pawn Stars* is filmed. Pat and I knew that it was in the opposite direction of where our hotel was and thought that we had literally just been taken for a ride. We were convinced that we would be stuck with the limo ride from downtown Vegas to the hotel. Even if the other group paid for the ride as far as Old Vegas, we were still going to have to pay for the ride all the way back, through rush hour to boot.

Pat and I sat silently (hard to believe, I know) and pondered how much this was going to set us back. We pulled out our wallets and started counting our cash to ensure we had enough to pay for the long journey back to the hotel.

We had almost arrived at the hotel when I asked Sam how much the limo ride was going to cost. He replied that the group he dropped off earlier at the Silver and Gold Shop had paid for the entire limo ride. What? That's crazy! Really? We left Sam a big fat tip and were overwhelmed with the generosity we had just experienced. We felt bad for thinking we got ripped off by the group we shared the limo with and turned grateful very quickly instead. Another amazing blessing!

The following day, we took a local bus to the Silver and Gold shop where *Pawn Stars* is filmed. Quite often, the owners of the shop are in the back or not on site, but this was not one of those days. We waited in line for approximately 20 minutes as they were filming an episode and only let a few people in the store at a time.

Pat's favorite cast member is Chumlee and as luck would have it, Chumlee was the only cast member working the counter that day. Both Pat and I chatted with him and had a photo taken. That was very cool. Very cool indeed!

The trip was unbelievable and we couldn't believe the timing of our visits to these popular TV show/real Las Vegas businesses.

Before we left Winnipeg, a friend of mine recommended a free show at one hotels located on the strip.

We meandered over there for the 2pm show, sat down, ordered a $10 beverage, and watched an incredible Elvis impersonator perform. He was amazing and sounded just like Elvis, and – had Elvis been 200 pounds heavier – he would have probably looked just like this impersonator.

As we're enjoying the show, who walks in? None other than the young fellow that hit on Pat in the shuttle bus the day we arrived. We got his attention and he sat with us until a dance contest was announced. They were asking for volunteers and Pat, along with this young buck, shot up their hands quicker than Quick Draw McGraw. They were now contestants in the dance competition. After several other couples also volunteered, the contest begun!

Pat and this young whippersnapper danced up a storm, step-by-step, stride-by-stride, never missing a beat, completely in time with each other. It was like they'd been dancing their entire life together. They never won the contest, which was a shame because they were the better dancers, hands-down!

Unfortunately, the young man was meeting up with his other colleagues and had to go. It was a shame for Pat as I think she was ready to take him out to the back 40 and show him that she was no <u>birdie</u>, as he affectionately referred to her in the shuttle, but rather a <u>cougar</u>, ready for some play time! Unfortunately, or maybe fortunately, he had friends waiting for him to head back to the convention and Pat was left hot-and-bothered, with no place to go.

Yes, indeed, the stars were aligned and Pat was walking around like a proud peacock ready to spread her feathers!

My brother-in-law Jim introduced me to a fabulous, old, Italian restaurant located a block off the Strip. Every meal is accompanied with unlimited red and white house wine. Pat and I had a reservation and were seated in a smaller area of the restaurant with only a couple of booths and a couple of two-seater tables.

After we attempted to make simple conversation with a fellow who was sitting by himself, we realized that he didn't want company or conversation. We gleefully moved onto another victim, who was much more friendly. The fellow was in Las Vegas on business. He worked in the hospitality industry and traveled a lot. He stayed at high-end hotels and was treated like royalty in hopes that these hotels would get a good review from him. In turn, the hotels would use the reviews to secure corporate accounts with large companies.

We joked around with him, mostly at Pat's expense.

I honestly don't know what got into me this trip but I had an arsenal of one-liners that I kept zinging at Pat. It's like I was having out of body experiences.

Pat found an opening and paid me back in spades. I made some kind of joke and the gentlemen said to Pat, "Your friend is pretty funny!"

I chimed in, "Ya, I'm all that and a bag of chips alright!" (as my sister June would say).

Not skipping a beat, Pat added, as she pointed at me circling her finger, "No, let's rephrase that. You're all that *because* of the bags of chips! Gotcha!" she said.

"Ooooh, nailed and target down!" I shouted out while laughing, almost falling off the bench.

Now some would have been completely insulted, but Pat owed me for so many one-liner comments throughout our trip, I had no problem accepting her stinger retort.

The fellow thought we were a travelling comedy show and the laughs kept on coming!

After dinner, we took in one show as previously mentioned in this story. *Menopause* had come highly recommended by a couple of my friends and it was age-appropriate for both Pat and I. *Menopause* is a live comedy performance of women going through "the phase" of night sweats, hot flashes, sex drive, weight gain and all the wonderful changes our bodies experience during this time. There were parts of the show where we laughed so hard I almost slid right out of my seat. One lady stopped us after the show and commented on how much fun she had watching us, as well as the show. We would highly recommend this show to anyone travelling to Vegas.

We had to wait for our shuttle to pick us up at the hotel and when it arrived, you would not believe who was on it! Yep, you guessed it! The very same group of guys from the Concrete Convention and they were primed! The howling began the second we got on the bus.

We had to make a pit stop for the boys to take a leak as one of them had to go so bad that he was going to pee in a one-litre bottle. With the shuttle bouncing all over the place, it's very likely that most of it would land on the floor. The bus driver took us to the old airport strip, stopped the bus, and waited for the boys to make their bladders gladder (a saying from my cousin Pearl).

At the airport, these young kids were stuck to us and wanted money to get something to eat, as they were flat broke. We helped them out and gave them a bite to eat to sober them up before they boarded their plane. We weren't convinced they would even be allowed on the plane in their condition. Turns out, they were sitting at the wrong gate and had missed their flight.

We, on the other hand, were completely sober as we had been all week.

On the plane ride home, we were punch-drunk. Like most of the trip, without a drop of alcohol in our systems, we could not stop laughing. We started to giggle as soon as we sat down in a much smaller aircraft than the one we flew down in. The seats were so squished together that my knees were practically touching the seat in front of me. I have a short body and short legs, therefore the space had to be very small for me to feel sandwiched in.

I was trying to get my headphone set out of my bag while balancing my purse and carry-on between my feet when I dropped the headphones on the floor. Since there was no room between my knees and the seat in front of me, I couldn't pick them up myself. I was sitting at the window and Pat was in the middle seat. Pat offered to pick them up as she could reach down to the side and grab them with her right hand. Even this was challenging, so I leaned towards the window picking up my left leg, making more room for Pat to slide sideways and grab them. Her head was essentially under my left butt cheek while reaching around for my ear buds.

While she was down there, I leaned down and said, "Olé!!"

I hadn't really farted, but I didn't tell her that until she was back up in her seat again.

Again, the makeup was running down our faces and we were literally out of control. We created quite a ruckus and since we hadn't pushed out of the gate yet, we were surprised that we weren't removed from the plane.

After we regained our composure, I took my ear bud and started speaking into it.

"MI60, come in MI60. MI48 here," I said. "Mission Control has ordered us back to Las Vegas every year from here-on-in. Should you accept this mission, you are required to be ready to respond to every one-liner comment in kind and be ready to go on short notice," I continued.

Pat responded by talking into her ear buds as if it were as natural as breathing. The conversation continued for several minutes with bursts of laughter in between.

I'm sure the other people on the plane thought we were on something, but we weren't. This trip involved very little alcohol and it was just pure fun and spontaneous moments, which made this trip magic!

When we finally arrived in Winnipeg, we made our way to the parkade to pick up Pat's vehicle. Pat dropped me off at home at 1:45am and I was greeted with the task of shoveling the entire sidewalk. The snow had not stopped since I had left and Dave was up north, leaving nobody to take care of our place.

The back gate was snow-blown shut and the snow was deep. I literally had to muscle the gate open, find the shovel, and then start the 20 minute process of clearing the sidewalk and deck so I could get into the house.

The next day, Pat called and told me that she only got home at 3am as she took several wrong turns after leaving my house and got completely lost. A trip that should have taken 12 minutes and only covered two main streets took her over an hour.

Thankfully, she took things in stride and just laughed. After all, laughter started, continued, and ended this phenomenal trip to Las Vegas, which I will remember for years and years to come.

<u>Side note:</u> I made a special t-shirt for Pat after we returned home – check out the photo

"Vegas Unleashed" (front and back) t-shirt made for Pat

I'm Speeding Because I Have To Poop!

Pat McBride - Thank You and House Warming
(Written by Shawna)

Happy Housewarming dear friend
And thank you as well
For the overnight invite
At your new lake "hotel"

I'm thrilled to be here
And can't wait to kick butt
On your set of dominos
And in your new hut

I miss you in Pinawa
But know this is your home
Next time it your turn
In Pioneer Bay to roam

Enjoy the small gifts
One, I KNOW you can use
To attempt to crush
Your "domino muse"

Shawna J Peterson

Ode to Roger Beebe
(As He Departs Civil Aviation)
(Written by Shawna)

Back In January 2004
You opened a door
And a new beginning was to start
Come to Civ. Av.
For you, we must have
And Civ. Av, I was now a part

The change was immense
Working the other side of the fence
But apparently work wasn't the only chore
You want "what" every morning
Roger I find you adoring
But coffee I do not make, nor pour

With binders stacked high
Darn near reaching the sky
Never in my life have I seen
"File this…file that"
"Find me this…find me that"
I named myself the Binder Queen

"Where's' Wayne" you shout
As I search all about
While doing 20 things at one time
"Call Gerri on the phone"
"Tell her I'm on my way home"
"But before I go, let's have a glass of wine"

I'm Speeding Because I Have To Poop!

I worked like a squirrel
Usually in a whirl
Collecting work like squirrels does nuts
When you went away
There was no time to play
As those nuts drove me nuckn' futs!!

With a bit of a rough start
I saw the kindest heart
From one of the gentler men I know
You were a pleasure to work for
I wish I could have done more
And now it's time for you to go

Good luck upstairs
Don't lose the rest of your hair
It's only a job you see
We're always here
To spread some good cheer
And you'll always be special to me

Shawna J Peterson

Ray's - 60th Birthday
(Written by Shawna)

There was a young named Ray
Who was wishing for a roll in the hay
Instead his friends from the lake
Have come to celebrate
His very special 60th birthday (sorry Ray...no nookie nookie)

Your expressions are legend
And your shorts are tradition
If your "shooters" were "hooters"
You'd never go fishin'

So here's to you, Ray
Our buddy.... Our friend!
Happy birthday you ole fart
Remember ... We're just around the bend!!

I'm Speeding Because I Have To Poop!

Good friends, Carole and Ray Dupuis, in Rincon de Guayabitos, Mexico

Shawna J Peterson

Carole's - 65th Birthday:
(Written by Shawna)

There once was a lady named Carole-Lee
Who said "I'm not 65...no not me"!
I look way too young
As she stuck out her tongue
While she gave us a "flash" for free

Now Roxy decided it was time
To show that she was still in her prime
Hoisted her dress
That showed mammary flesh
And said "next time I'll charge you a dime"

Well she sure proved us wrong
As she sported her thong
And stuck her finger in the air
Be damned with the number
And left us with wonder
"kiss me arse...65? WHO CARES"!

I'm Speeding Because I Have To Poop!

Carole's - 67th Birthday
(Written by Shawna)

Roses are red
Violets are blue
Carole may be 67
But she still looks good as new

Roses are red
Lilies are white
Even at 67
She's still DY-NO-MITE

Roses are red
Pansies are pink
It's called a medical condition now
When your farts stink (you can get away with it now!!)

Roses are red
Marigolds are gold (duh)
Even though your 67
You're not even close to being old

Shawna J Peterson

Uncle Ben's 80th Birthday
(Written by Shawna)

We celebrate your birthday
And for me it's hard to believe
That my very special uncle Ben
80 years ago was conceived

Now I know I'm still a baby
Next to your wise ole years
But allow me to share a bit of advice
Over one or two celebratory beers

The body changes as we age
And at 80, I'd say you're getting pretty close
So take all the meds that are available to you
And try not forgetting a dose

Now eating is also important you know
Especially when you're thin as a rail
So indulge in some baking and other goodies too
As man cannot live on rye and ginger ale

Energy is something you must conserve
And sleeping is critical too
Try to relax and not get stressed out
And keep a positive point of view

One more piece of advice I must give
I hope I'm not out of line
But this next one is "THE" most important one
And this opinion is solely mine

I'm Speeding Because I Have To Poop!

At times you may feel 100
And other times younger and full of zeal
But always remember, ole dear Uncle Ben
"You're only as old as the <u>woman</u> you feel" ☺

Chapter VI

Concerts / Live Performances

Music has always been a very big part of my life. Whether it was singing in the church choir or attending live performances, I loved to hear music in all formats. In addition to the concerts and events below, I also enjoyed numerous live theatre productions in Winnipeg, Toronto and Las Vegas.

The concerts and performances I attended with my nieces **Cheyenne and Jamie** are precious memories I hold dear. Instead of birthday gifts, the girls and I would make a date for a live event. They always got to pick which event they wanted to see and I would provide the ticket. Our date nights to celebrate their birthdays were fun and sometimes included a sleepover too. For the most part, we had similar taste in music and only on a couple of occasions, should I have received "Auntie of the Year" award. Can you guess which ones they are?

Concert	**Went With**
Adam Lambert	Teresa
Alan Jackson	Dave, Mom and Dad
Alice Cooper	Colleague
Beach Boys	Friend
Beatle-Mania	Joanie
Bette Midler (x2)	Dave, June and Nancy
Bob Dylan	Dave and **Cheyenne**

Concert	Went With
Bruno Mars	Wendy
Burton Cummings	Pearl
Carrie Underwood	June
Charlie Major	Teresa, Dave and Dad
Chris de Burgh (2x)	Friend, and Robyn
Dixie Chicks	Alone
Doc Walker	Teresa
Eagles	Janet
Hunter Hayes	June
Janelle Monet	**Jamie**
John Fogerty	Dave
Johnny Reid	Dave
Jonas Brothers	**Jamie**
Journey	Friend
Justin Bieber	**Jamie**
Il Divo (x2)	Transport Canada ladies, and Darlyn
Katy Perry	**Jamie**
Kenny Rogers	June
Lady Gaga	June
Meatloaf	Debbie
Michael Buble´	Dave and Cheryl
Nazareth	Friend
Neil Diamond	Unsure
Pink	Teresa, Joanie, Rob, Sue, Justine, Madison, Kelsey
Queen	Teresa
Rascal Flatts	Dave
Rod Stewart (x 2)	Kathy, Cheryl and Valerie
Rush	Friend
Selena Gomez	**Jamie**
Shania Twain	Group of Transport Canada ladies
Sir Elton John	Cheryl

I'm Speeding Because I Have To Poop!

Concert	**Went With**
Sir Paul McCartney	Sunny 'D' (aka Deanna)
Tran-Siberian Orchestra	Sue
Taylor Swift	**Jamie and her girlfriend**
The Mavericks	Dave
The Rankin Family (x 2)	Dave, and Wilma
Toby Keith	Dave
Yes	Friend

Other Live Events/Musicals:	**Went With**
Cavalia - Odysseo	Dave
Part VIICirque de Soleil (3 shows)	**Cheyenne**, Wilma, and Nancy
Disney on Ice (several shows)	**Cheyenne and Jamie**
Ice Capades (several shows)	**Cheyenne and Mom 'P'**
Joseph and the Dream Coat (x2)	Mom, and Andrea
Lord of the Dance	Dave and Mom 'P'
Mamma Mia (x2)	Andrea, Ken and Louise with Kathy
Menopause	Pat
Stars on Ice	**Cheyenne and Jamie**
Winnie the Pooh – Live	**Jamie**
William Shatner	Lindsay

Thank You!

Thank you for taking the time to read this silly little book capturing a few snippets of the Derksen family, along with periods in my own life with family and friends. I hope you have enjoyed the tidbits of information, much of it containing embarrassing moments life can throw at us.

The publishing company I initially worked with indicated that the Derksen family was willing to share much more with complete strangers, than most families would even share amongst themselves.

Thankfully, the Derksen family doesn't take life's imperfect moments too seriously and most often, is able to laugh them off. When bad decisions are made or life throws us to the curb, we kick into recovery mode and get back up. After brushing off the dust, and having a little laugh or cry, we make amends, and then move on. With any luck, we've learned something along the way too!

While this is a humourous look at our family, it is that very premise of being imperfect and the recovery process, which has tested our strength and resilience, especially in moments of crisis and loss. I am incredibly proud to be a Derksen and blessed beyond measure to have amazing family members and friends in my life!

During the process of writing this book, family and friends have mentioned other funny and embarrassing stories that have made us laugh till we cried, and suggested another book be written. I've started collecting more true stories and poems for the second book in the "Dumping with the Derksen's" series.

I'll leave you with these parting words that, thanks to my awesome church family, I learned and now live by every day ~

<u>Remember to Always:</u>
- ❖ Love with all your heart
- ❖ Accept people the way they are
- ❖ Forgive quickly
- ❖ **<u>Laugh</u>** often (even if it's at yourself!)

God bless you all!

With love, thanks and gratitude,
Shawna

www.ingramcontent.com/pod-product-compliance
Lightning Source LLC
LaVergne TN
LVHW051554070426
835507LV00021B/2577